STRONGMAN

WRITER
Charles Soule

ARTIST
Allen Gladfelter

COVERS
Paul Adam

STRONGMAN LOGO
John Rubio

ORIGINAL CONCEPT
Charles Soule and Andrew Deemer

Special Thanks To: Amy and Rosemary Soule, Andrew Deemer, Ian Horowitz, Shawn Hynes, Carl Marcellino, Caitlin Mock-Marcellino, Shawn DePasquale, Thommy Melanson, Michael Pereira, B. Clay Moore, Joshua Hale Fialkov, Jimmy Palmiotti, Brad Meltzer and all the friends and family who gave encouragement and insight. All of you made this book possible.

Published by SLG Publishing
P.O. Box 26427
San Jose, CA 95159

www.slgcomic.com

First Printing: March 2009
ISBN-13: 978-1-59362-152-0

WELCOME BACK TO DAY FOUR OF THE SIXTH ANNUAL LUCHADOR WEEK ON CHANNEL 59'S BIG MORNING MOVIE!
PLUNDER MY LANDS?
NNNGH
THIS YEAR, OF COURSE, WE'RE CELEBRATING THE CAREER OF ONE OF THE GREATEST OF THE SOUTH-OF-THE-BORDER MASKED WRESTLER HEROES...
¡TIGRE!
WE KICKED THINGS OFF ON MONDAY WITH ONE OF THE BIG MAN'S EARLIEST FILMS, "TIGRE VS. THE CORONADO CABAL."
GO BACK TO YOUR QUEEN. TELL HER THIS PLACE IS PROTECTED!!
ALLEN GLADFELTER
6

SSSSSSS
AIEEEEEE!!
IF YOU'RE THAT HUNGRY, YOU BLOOD-SUCKING PUTA...
PERHAPS YOU'D PREFER SOME STAKE!!
TUESDAY BROUGHT YOU ANOTHER LANDMARK IN THE CAREER OF THIS WEEK'S FEATURED HERO, 1967'S "TIGRE IN: THE VAMPIRE WHORE."
THE PICTURE FEATURED THE INTRODUCTION OF THE FIRST OF TIGRE'S TWO LOYAL COMRADES-IN-ARMS, A BRASH YOUNG WEAPONS MASTER KNOWN AS...
¡CONEJO!

PREPARE TO BURN, TIGRE! YOU AND YOUR BUNNY BUDDY!
SORRY TO DISAPPOINT...
NO!!!
...COOKOUT'S CANCELLED.
BETTER LUCK NEXT TIME, BUG MAN.
TIGRE'S CLASSIC TEAM CAME TOGETHER JUST A YEAR LATER IN THE LANDMARK "TIGRE Y LA FURIA DEL SEÑOR ESCARABAJO."
FOR THOSE OF YOU WHO DON'T SPEAK SPANISH, THAT'S "TIGRE AND THE ANGER OF MISTER BEETLE."
AND HERE WE MET THE FINAL MEMBER OF THE TRIO. AN OLDER GENTLEMAN, ALWAYS DAPPER IN HIS OFF-THE-SHOULDER TUNIC, ALWAYS READY WITH JUST THE RIGHT INVENTION TO SAVE THE DAY, THE WISE, BRILLIANT...
¡BUJO!

TIGRE IS NOT AS WELL-KNOWN IN THE U.S. AS SOME OF THE OTHER LUCHADOR HEROES, SUCH AS THE IMMORTAL EL SANTO.
HOWEVER, HIS CAREER STANDS UP TO THE BEST: A LEGACY OF MORE THAN FORTY ENTERTAINING FILMS, AN ASTONISHING 200-1-1 RECORD IN THE RING,
AND PERSISTENT RUMORS THAT HE SPENT HIS PERSONAL TIME FIGHTING CRIME ON BEHALF OF THE CITIZENS OF MEXICO.
“ESTO ES UN TRABAJO PARA
BUJO Y CONEJO”, AFIRMO
LIKE THE OTHER LEGENDS OF THE GENRE, HE NEVER REMOVED HIS MASK IN PUBLIC, NOR DID EITHER OF HIS COLLEAGUES.
“SIEMPRE SERA
SO WHY CAN'T YOU FIND HIS MOVIES ON DVD? WHY DON'T HIPSTER BANDS WEAR HIS MASK, OR PUNK KIDS SPRAY-PAINT IT ON THE SIDEWALK?
ALLEN GLADFELTER

¡TIGRE
EL LUCHADOR
No.1
TIGRE
THE ANSWER MAY LIE IN THE FACT THAT THIRTY YEARS AGO THIS FRIDAY, TIGRE, BUJO AND CONEJO DISAPPEARED WITHOUT A TRACE, AT THE HEIGHT OF THEIR FAME. NO MORE FILMS, NO WRESTLING MATCHES, NOTHING. WHERE DID TIGRE GO? WHY WOULD A MAN WITH EVERYTHING JUST WALK AWAY?
LIBRE
GRE VS
E NEGRO
A MANO ESPECIAL
Y LOS AMIGOS CON TIGRE
BUJO Y CONEJO
VS.
EL VIKINGO Y ASTRO REY
ARENA
SAN JUAN
DE FEB
THE REASONS REMAIN SHROUDED IN THE MISTS OF MASKED WRESTLER HISTORY. BUT HERE AT LUCHADOR WEEK, WE ARE DEDICATED TO NOT LETTING THE MEMORY OF HEROES LIKE TIGRE FADE.
SO STAY TUNED, FANS! RETURN WITH US TO A SIMPLER TIME, WHEN GIANT LIZARD-MEN WALKED THE EARTH, AND STRONG MEN IN WRESTLING MASKS KEPT US SAFE FROM THEM.
AMA TAN HERMOSA"
ctuar como "cientif-

COMING UP NEXT, IT'S "TIGRE AND THE DANCE OF THE DINOSAUR PEOPLE!"
¡TIGRE!

WHAT THE HELL IS THIS ON THE TV?

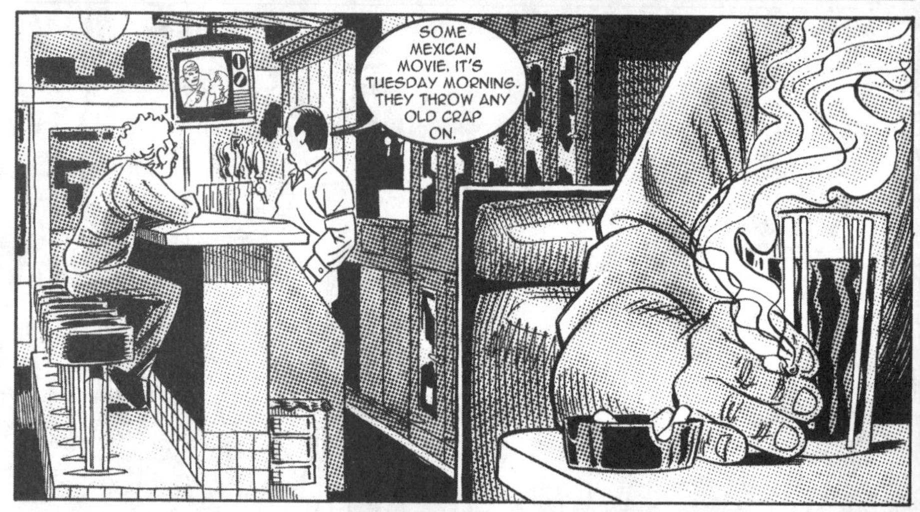
SOME MEXICAN MOVIE. IT'S TUESDAY MORNING. THEY THROW ANY OLD CRAP ON.

THIS IS SOME RIDICULOUS SHIT.

COME ON, MAN, MAYBE THERE'S A GAME ON.
YOU WANNA WATCH SOMETHING ELSE, YOU CAN PAY TO GET CABLE IN HERE.

OLD GRAND DAD 7 BOURBON
IF YOU ACTUALLY THINK I'M DRAGGING MY ASS UP ON A STOOL TO CHANGE THE CHANNEL FOR YOU, MAYBE I NEED TO CUT YOU OFF EARLY.
THIS IS SOME RIDICULOUS SHIT, THAT'S ALL I'M SAYIN'.

ABUELLA'S MARKET
ORGE
ELGADO
COUNCIL

<HIC>

WHYN'T YOU WATCH WHERE YOU GOIN?
WHATHEFUCK, BITCH!
SORRY, SORRY.

PENDEJO BETTER **WATCH** HIMSELF!

LEARN A LITTLE **RESPECT** FOR HIS BETTERS!

JORGE DELGADO
FOR CITY COUNCIL
CHANGE
JORGE DELGADO
CITY COUNCIL
CHAN

<HIC>
EXIT
...MIERDA...

KRRRACK!
MIERDA!

MALDITO SEA!
I SEE YOU, YOU OLD DRUNK! YOU CAN'T TELL ME SOMEONE WAS TRYING TO BREAK IN THIS TIME!
THIS IS YOUR LAST CHANCE.

NEXT TIME IT HAPPENS YOU'RE EVICTED!
AND YOU'RE PAYING FOR THAT DOOR!

<HOW CAN THIS HAVE HAPPENED?>*
*TRANSLATED FROM SPANISH.
MEXICO, 1973.
<THE TONE OF THE RANSOM NOTE SUGGESTS WE ARE FAMILIAR WITH THE KIDNAPPER, BUT I CANNOT IMAGINE WHO...
...EVEN OUR MOST DIABOLICAL ENEMIES HAVE A SENSE OF HONOR. THIS IS *UGLI-NESS*.>
<DON'T WORRY, MY FRIEND. WE WILL GET HER BACK. THIS WILL NOT STAND.>
<IT *CANNOT* STAND!>
<WHAT ARE WE WAITING FOR? LET US GO. LET US MEET THIS ENEMY, AND TEACH HIM WHAT IT MEANS TO GO AGAINST US!>
<YES!>
<MY FRIENDS, PERHAPS WE SHOULD PAUSE TO CONSIDER BEFORE WE ACT. WE MAY NOT COMPLETE-LY UNDERSTAND WHAT IS HAPPEN-ING HERE.>
<AH, BUJO, YOUR AGE IS SHOWING! NO, CONEJO IS RIGHT. WE WILL DO WHAT WE HAVE ALWAYS DONE. WE WILL *FIGHT!*
AND WHEN OUR ENEMY IS VANQUISHED AND THE WORLD IS BRIGHT AGAIN, WE WILL LAUGH AT YOUR CAUTION.>
KNOCK KNOCK
EHH?
KNOCK KNOCK

KNOCK KNOCK

URRRRRGH.

UNO MOMENTO!

HELLO? MR. TIGRE?

OH, THANK GOODNESS! PLEASE, SIR, I MUST SPEAK TO YOU. MY NAME IS MARIA. MAY I COME IN?
HOW...? HOW CAN YOU BE HERE?
I AM SORRY, I DON'T THINK WE HAVE MET BEFORE TO-NIGHT, MR. TIGRE.
AHH... YES, OF COURSE. MY MISTAKE. BUT HOW DO YOU KNOW THE NAME TIGRE? NO ONE HAS CALLED ME THAT FOR MANY YEARS.
MY MOTHER TOLD ME STORIES OF YOU WHEN I WAS A CHILD, AND SHOWED ME YOUR FILMS.
I SAW YOU IN THE NEIGHBOR-HOOD, AND KNEW IT HAD TO BE YOU. WHO *ELSE* WOULD DARE TO WEAR YOUR MASK, MR. TIGRE?
PLEASE. IT IS JUST TIGRE. IF YOU MUST CALL ME THAT, USE IT AS IT WAS USED.
I WILL. BUT NOW, MAY I COME IN?
IF YOU LIKE. BUT I MUST GO TO WORK SOON, SO YOU WILL NEED TO SPEAK QUICKLY.
DID SOMEONE BREAK IN?
...YES.
THEN I PITY THAT MAN. SURELY NOW HE HAS NOTHING BUT REGRET.
SURELY.
IT MUST BE A SIGN THAT I SAW YOU ON THE STREET.
GONE FOR SO *LONG*, AND JUST AS YOUR PEOPLE NEED YOU ONCE AGAIN, YOU APPEAR.
I LEFT MEXICO FOR A *REASON*, YOUNG LADY.
I CAME TO THE CITY TO LEAVE THAT LIFE BEHIND.
....
WHY ARE YOU HERE?

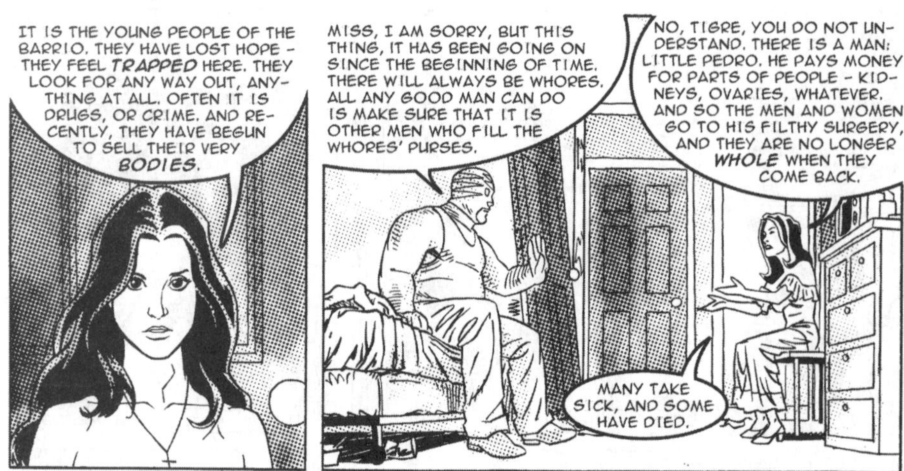
IT IS THE YOUNG PEOPLE OF THE BARRIO. THEY HAVE LOST HOPE - THEY FEEL TRAPPED HERE. THEY LOOK FOR ANY WAY OUT, ANYTHING AT ALL. OFTEN IT IS DRUGS, OR CRIME. AND RECENTLY, THEY HAVE BEGUN TO SELL THEIR VERY BODIES.
MISS, I AM SORRY, BUT THIS THING, IT HAS BEEN GOING ON SINCE THE BEGINNING OF TIME. THERE WILL ALWAYS BE WHORES. ALL ANY GOOD MAN CAN DO IS MAKE SURE THAT IT IS OTHER MEN WHO FILL THE WHORES' PURSES.
NO, TIGRE, YOU DO NOT UNDERSTAND. THERE IS A MAN: LITTLE PEDRO. HE PAYS MONEY FOR PARTS OF PEOPLE - KIDNEYS, OVARIES, WHATEVER. AND SO THE MEN AND WOMEN GO TO HIS FILTHY SURGERY, AND THEY ARE NO LONGER WHOLE WHEN THEY COME BACK.
MANY TAKE SICK, AND SOME HAVE DIED.

THIS IS A SAD STORY, MARIA, BUT WHAT WOULD YOU HAVE ME DO? THESE PEOPLE CHOOSE TO MAKE THESE BARGAINS. AND ULTIMATELY, IT HELPS PEOPLE, DOES IT NOT? EVERY KIDNEY SOLD GOES TO SAVE THE LIFE OF SOMEONE WHO NEEDS IT.
BUT FOR EACH PIECE OF THEMSELVES THEY LET BE CARVED AWAY, THEY LOSE PART OF THEIR SOUL... THEIR HOPE. AND WITHOUT HOPE, LIFE SEEMS WORTH SO LITTLE, WHY NOT TRADE SOME OF IT AWAY FOR A FEW THOUSAND DOLLARS? THEY SEE IT AS A FAIR DEAL, TIGRE!
AGAIN, I ASK YOU, WHAT WOULD YOU HAVE ME DO? EVEN IF I WERE STILL AS I ONCE WAS, HOW CAN I CHANGE THINGS?

YOU ARE TIGRE.
IF PEOPLE HERE LACK HOPE AND STRENGTH, WHO BETTER TO GIVE IT TO THEM? SIR, YOU ARE HOPE AND STRENGTH.
MY MOTHER TOLD ME THAT BACK IN MEXICO, YOU WERE NOT JUST A FILM STAR AND WRESTLER. YOU SOLVED CRIMES, FOUGHT EVIL EVERYWHERE IT COULD BE FOUND.
IF PEOPLE SAW YOU ACTIVE AGAIN, INVESTIGATING, TRYING TO MAKE THE WORLD A BETTER PLACE, THEY WOULD BE INSPIRED TO FIND SOMETHING BETTER FOR THEMSELVES. I KNOW IT.
I AM FLATTERED THAT IN YOUR YOUTH YOU SEE SO MUCH IN ME, MARIA. BUT THE TRUTH IS SIMPLE, AND YOU WILL LEARN IT AS YOU AGE.
IF YOU ARE RICH, ONE DAY YOU WILL BE POOR. IF ONCE YOU LOVE, SOME DAY YOU WILL MOURN.
AND IF ONCE YOU ARE TIGRE, YOU BECOME...
...THIS.

YOU ARE STILL EVERYTHING YOU WERE, TIGRE. I CAN SEE IT IN YOU, EVEN IF YOU CAN'T. *PLEASE*, JUST PROMISE ME THAT YOU WILL LOOK INTO THIS.
I CANNOT INVOLVE MY-SELF. I AM SORRY, BUT I AM AN OLD MAN.
MY LIFE IS SMALL, BUT I DO NOT WISH TO RISK WHAT LITTLE I HAVE GETTING MIXED UP IN GANGSTER BUSINESS.

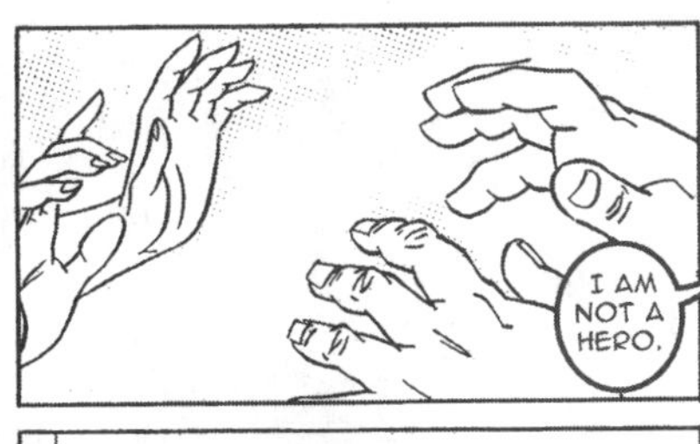
I AM NOT A HERO.

AND NOW I MUST GO TO WORK. I AM SORRY THAT YOU HAVE WASTED YOUR TIME.

PLEASE, SIR. I HAVE SAVED $300 FROM MY WORK. IF YOU WILL JUST TRY, EVEN IF YOU FIND NOTHING, YOU CAN HAVE IT ALL.

YOUR MONEY WOULD BE WASTED ON ME.

IF YOU CHANGE YOUR MIND, I WORK AT THE FLOWER STAND ON NATIONAL AVENUE.
I HOPE I WILL SEE YOU AGAIN, TIGRE. THIS IS NOT WHO YOU ARE.

HEY HEY, THERE'S MY FAVORITE RUDO!
YOU READY, BIG GUY? ALMOST SHOW-TIME.

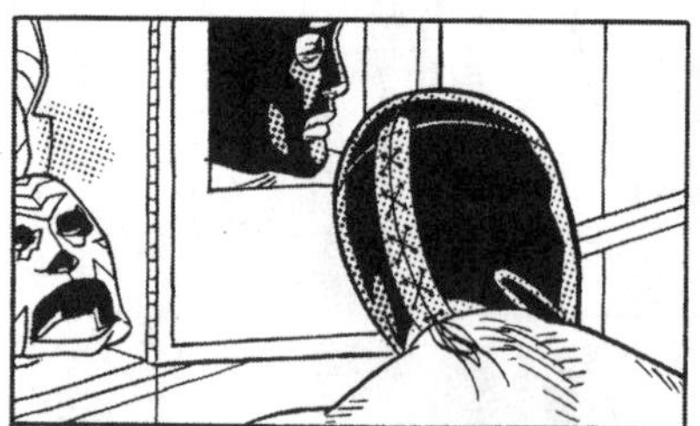

WHO IS IT TONIGHT?
ARENA
TONIGHT, PAL, YOU'RE GOING UP AGAINST THE SLUGGER. SHOULD BE A GREAT SHOW. PEOPLE LOVE THAT GUY.

THE SLUGGER?

YOU GOT IT. JUST DO WHAT YOU ALWAYS DO. YOU GET THE SHIT KICKED OUT OF YOU BETTER THAN ANY-ONE I EVER SEEN. JUST DO WHAT COMES NATURAL.

MUST HE USE THE BAT TONIGHT? EVERYTHING ELSE CAN BE DONE IN A WAY THAT THE HURT GOES AWAY...
BUT THE BAT, THAT *LASTS*.
GOOD ONE, BIG MAN.
LIKE ANYTHING COULD HURT *YOU*.
BESIDES, YOU KNOW THE BASEBALL BAT FINISHING MOVE IS SLUGGER'S SIGNATURE. PEOPLE DON'T GET THAT, THEY DON'T FEEL THEY GET THEIR MONEY'S WORTH.

PLEASE, MR. GREEN. JUST ASK HIM. MAYBE HE WILL CONSIDER IT.

LISTEN, YOU STUPID OLD SON OF A BITCH. IF I TELL YOU SLUGGER'S GONNA SHOVE THAT BAT UP YOUR ASS TONIGHT, YOU'RE GOING TO *LUBE UP* AND *SPREAD!*
YOU WANT YOUR FIFTY BUCKS, YOU DON'T FUCK AROUND.
FUCK AROUND, AND TOMORROW NIGHT IT'S SOME OTHER SAD BASTARD GETTING THAT FIFTY BUCKS INSTEAD OF YOU.

GET UP TO THE RING. I NEED YOU THERE FOR SLUGGER'S ENTRANCE.
ARENA

ARENA

ARENA
KRUNCH!

ARENA

LADIES AND GENTLEMEN! WELCOME TO TUESDAY NIGHT THROWDOWN AT THE UPTOWN ARENA!
LET ME HEAR IT- YOU READY FOR SOME *PAIN*?
WELL, OUR GLADIATORS WILL DO THEIR BEST TO OBLIGE! AND SPEAKING OF THAT, YOU'VE HAD ENOUGH OF ME, I'M SURE.
LET'S GET READY FOR SOME ACTION!
RAAH!
YEAH!
HOOAH!
IT'S A *GREAT* CARD TONIGHT!
FOR THE FIRST MATCH, WE'VE GOT ONE OF YOUR FAVORITES.
BUT BEFORE WE BRING HIM OUT, LET ME INTRODUCE HIS OPPONENT. YOU KNOW HIM, YOU HATE HIM...
...IN THE BLUE CORNER, THE BLACK DEMON!!
BOO!

HISS!
PERDEDOR!
BOO!
...FATTY!

BOO!
... SO *OLD*! IT'S ALMOST SAD!
AND ENTERING THROUGH THE WEST DOORS...
...IT'S THE TWO- TIME SOUTHERN LEAGUE CHAMPION, THE MAN TOO HARD-CORE FOR THE MAJOR LEAGUES, HERE FOR YOU TONIGHT...

RAHHH!
YES!
LOVE YOU!
THE SLUGGER!

BEAT HIS ASS!
KILL HIM!

OKAY, BOYS, LET'S GIVE 'EM WHAT THEY CAME FOR.
SLUGGER, DON'T KILL HIM, ALL RIGHT?
AS LONG AS HE DON'T FORGET THE MOVES, AIN'T NOBODY GETTING KILLED.

YOU REMEMBER THE MOVES, OLD MAN?

YO... RECUERDO.*
*"I... remember."

SPEAK ENGLISH. THIS IS AMERICA.

THUD!
UNGH!!
OH, I'M SORRY, WAS THAT BEFORE THE BELL?
DING DING!
GIVE ME SOMETHING TO WORK WITH! THESE FOLKS PAID TO SEE THIS!
WHAMMO!
PATHETIC! NEXT TIME...
...I HOPE THEY GIVE ME A FIGHTER WORTH MY TIME!
RRAAARGH!
OOF!
WATCH YOURSELF, OLD MAN.

YAAAAAAH!
1... 2...
THOUGHT YOU'D GET CUTE, EH?
NOT SMART, PAL. NOT SMART...
...AT ALL!
BAT!
DO IT!
YEEAH!
NNNH.
FINISH HIM!
BAT!
SLAM!

AND A ONE,
AND A TWO,
AND A...

...SEE YA!!
THWOCK!!
AUUGH!

SLUGGER!
HELL YESSS!
HIT HIM AGAIN!

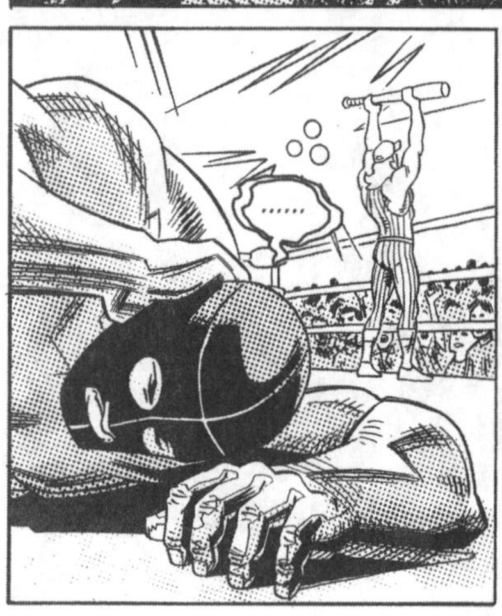
......

THIS
IS NOT WHO
YOU ARE.

NO...
WHAT THE HELL, MAN?

HEY!
...MORE...

...BAT!!
YOU MAY WALK OUT OF THIS RING NOW...

OR WE WILL GO ANOTHER ROUND...
AND YOUR FRIENDS WILL HAVE TO CARRY YOU OUT.

BOO!
COME ON!

CULO!
...MONEY BACK...

YOU'RE *FINISHED*, YOU DUMB FUCKER!
WHAT THE HELL WERE YOU THINKING?

YOU GET YOUR SHIT AND GET OUT!
I NEVER WANT TO SEE YOU DOWN HERE AGAIN.
AND I'M GOING TO CALL THE OTHER RINGS AROUND TOWN - YOU'RE *THROUGH*.
YOU HEAR ME?
FIFTY DOLLARS.

ARE YOU OUT OF YOUR GODDAMNED MIND? I'M NOT PAYING YOU *ANYTHING* FOR THAT PERFORMANCE! THAT WAS A...THAT WAS A *TRAVESTY*.
I WILL NOT ASK AGAIN.

TAKE IT AND GET OUT. CHRIST.

GRACIAS.

GOLD
DIAMONDS
WATCHES
Frank's PAPAYA
PAPAYA
PAPAYA
JACKSON
HEWITT
SUBWAY

125TH
NATIONAL AVE
WALK

MARIA.

I *KNEW* I WOULD SEE YOU AGAIN.
I... APOLOGIZE FOR NOT TAKING YOUR OFFER SERIOUSLY BEFORE.
WILL YOU ALLOW AN OLD FOOL THE OPPORTUNITY TO RECONSIDER?

MUST YOU EVEN ASK?

I CANNOT PROMISE THAT I WILL FIND ANYTHING, BUT I WILL LOOK INTO THIS MAN YOU TOLD ME OF.

HIS NAME IS LITTLE PEDRO.
HE RUNS A STRIP CLUB AT THE CORNER OF CHAVEZ AND STATE. HIS SURGERY IS IN THE BASEMENT.
YOU SHOULD FIND HIM THERE.
THEN THAT IS WHERE I SHALL BEGIN.

HERE, FOR LUCK.

MARIA, THANK YOU FOR THE FLOWER.
ITS BEAUTY IS SURPASSED ONLY BY YOUR OWN LOVELINESS.
BUT YOU HAD MENTIONED A SUM IN OUR EARLIER DISCUSSION - 300 DOLLARS?

OF COURSE, OF COURSE, I AM SO STUPID TO HAVE FORGOTTEN.

HERE YOU ARE.
THREE HUNDRED, AS WE AGREED.
I AM SURE YOU WILL EARN EVERY CENT.
A THOUSAND THANKS. I WILL BEGIN IN THE MORNING, AND YOU WILL SEE ME AGAIN SOON.

NO TRESPASSING

VROOM!
RUMMMBLE
NO TRESPASSING

RUMMBLE

HEY MISTER! NICE BIKE!

THANK YOU, SON. GET INSIDE NOW. YOU DON'T WANT TO FALL.

R-R ROOM!!
BYE, MISTER!

SHIT, WHO THE HELL THIS DUDE SUPPOSED TO BE?
THAT'S ANDRE THE GIANT, MAN.
ISLANDS

NAH, MAN. THAT GUY'S DEAD.
DEAD MY ASS! HE'S RIGHT THERE. AND MY MAN ANDRE GOT HIM ONE HELL OF A RIDE.
BAD BRAIN

I'M SORRY, SIR, PERHAPS YOU DIDN'T SEE THE SIGN? THERE'S NO PARKING IN FRONT OF THE CLUB. YOU'LL WANT TO LEAVE IT WITH THE VALET.
BAD BRAINS

NO PARKING
DROP OFFS PICK UPS ONLY
VALET PARKING ON STATE ST
-$15.00-

TINK!

ISLANDS
DON'T TOUCH THE BIKE.

WHAT CAN I GET YOU, FRIEND?
I AM HERE TO SEE LITTLE PEDRO.

HE AIN'T HERE, BUT I'LL PASS ALONG A MESSAGE.
WHAT DO YOU NEED HIM FOR?

TELL HIM I AM HERE TO MAKE A SALE. I HAVE HEARD HE WILL PAY WELL FOR ITEMS OF GOOD QUALITY.

GOOD QUALITY, EH? TO BE HONEST, PAL, YOU LOOK A LITTLE THE WORSE FOR WEAR. BUT HEY, IF LP WANTS TO BUY, THAT'S HIS BUSINESS.
HE'S IN THE BACK. RIGHT THROUGH THOSE DOORS.
GRACIAS.

HEY THERE, FRIEND. OTIS JUST BUZZED ME.

LITTLE PEDRO
SAID YOU WANTED TO DO SOME BUSINESS?

IN FRONT OF THE LADY?
OH, DON'T MIND ME!
YEAH, DON'T MIND HER. HAVE A SEAT- WE'LL TALK.

SO, YOU'RE HERE TO DROP A LITTLE WEIGHT THE EASY WAY, EH?
SO WHAT I HAVE HEARD IS TRUE. YOU PAY MONEY FOR PEOPLE'S ORGANS.
TOO BAD I DON'T BUY FAT. YOU'D WALK OUT OF HERE A RICH MAN.

TRUE? BROTHER, THAT'S AS TRUE AS MY FEELINGS FOR MY SWEET-HEART HERE.
AWW, HON, THAT'S SO NICE.
A VERY OLD MAN WITH ENORMOUS WINGS

JUST SPEAKING FROM THE HEART, DARLING.
BUT YES, SIR, I DO ENGAGE IN THAT TRADE. JUST HAVE A LOOK AT MY MENU HERE.
MENU
KIDNEY - $8000
LIVER - $16,000
LUNG - $20,000
HEART - $24,000
ALL SALES FINAL
LITTLE PEDRO
I PAY WELL. NO-ONE WALKS OUT OF HERE FEELING CHEATED.

HELL, WE MIGHT EVEN BE ABLE TO WORK OUT A LITTLE DIS-COUNT.
DOROTHY AND I WERE JUST ABOUT TO DO A LITTLE DANCE OF THE CLOUDS AND RAIN. YOU WANT IN? MAKE US HAPPY, I'LL GIVE YOU THE FRIENDS AND FAMILY RATE.
WHAT DO YOU THINK, HON?

OH YEAH, NICE! BIG STRONG BULL LIKE THAT. WE HAVEN'T HAD A BIG GUY IN A LONG TIME.
JUST MAKE HIM KEEP THE MASK ON.

DEVIANTS! ENOUGH OF THIS FILTHY TALK. TELL ME NOW -- WHAT DO YOU DO WITH THE ORGANS YOU PURCHASE?
THEY GET TAKEN CARE OF, FREAK. WHAT DO YOU CARE, AS LONG AS YOU GET PAID?

I MUST INSIST.
WHAT HAPPENS TO THE ORGANS?

LISTEN, MAN.
I WAS DOWN WITH THE WHOLE MASK THING WHEN YOU CAME IN. I SAID TO MYSELF, 'THIS IS A MAN WHO UNDER-STANDS THAT STYLE ISN'T ALWAYS ABOUT WHAT'S TRADITIONAL.'
BUT NOW YOU'RE STARTING TO PISS ME OFF. IF YOU'RE HERE TO SELL SOME-THING, NAME THE PART AND I'LL NAME THE PRICE. OTHERWISE, GET THE FUCK OUT OF HERE AND LEAVE ME TO MY AFTERNOON TUMBLE.

I WILL GO NOWHERE UNTIL YOU ANSWER MY QUESTIONS.
AND IT WILL GO BETTER FOR YOU IF YOU ANSWER THEM NOW, INSTEAD OF LATER.
SO NOW YOU'RE THREATENING ME IN FRONT OF MY WOMAN? THAT'S TERRIBLE, MAN.

CLIP, I NEED YOU IN HERE, MAN. NOW.
BIG PEDRO
RIGHT AWAY, BOSS.

GET THIS NUT OUT OF HERE. HE'S PUTTING ME OFF MY GAME.
WITH PLEASURE, BOSS.

I DO NOT BELIEVE WE WERE INTRO-DUCED, WHEN WE MET OUT-SIDE.

I AM TIGRE.

CLIP.

RRRRRRRGH!

MMMMMMMPH!

KRAAACK!

AAOO-OWWW!

UHH, LISTEN, DOROTHY BABY... CAN OUR SPECIAL TIME WAIT A FEW MINUTES? DADDY'S GOT TO TALK SOME BUSINESS.
AWW... MAKE IT QUICK, OK, HONEY?
SURE THING, BABY. SURE THING.

THIS IS THE LAST TIME I WILL ASK YOU BEFORE YOU FEEL MY FISTS.
WHERE DO THE ORGANS GO?
NO NEED FOR THAT ACTION, FRIEND. I'LL TELL YOU.
I PUT THEM IN A COOLER, PACKED WITH DRY ICE, RIGHT?
THERE'S A GUY, CARL. OTIS TAKES HIM THE COOLERS, GETS PAID AND BRINGS THE MONEY BACK HERE.

WHERE?

DOWNTOWN. I CAN GIVE YOU THE ADDRESS.
YES, YOU'LL DO THAT. A COOLER IS READY NOW?
OTIS HAS ONE, OUT IN THE BAR. HE'S GOING TO DELIVER IT TODAY.

I WILL MAKE YOUR DELIVERY. THE ADDRESS?
211 WEST ALMODOVAR. IT'S A PIZZA PLACE.
BUT WHAT ABOUT MY MONEY, MAN? YOU TAKE THAT COOLER, YOU'RE GOING TO OWE ME.

RIGHT. YEAH. JUST KIDDING.

YOU WILL STOP THIS BUSINESS. NO MORE BUYING BODY PARTS. FIND ANOTHER WAY TO MAKE MONEY.
DO NOT CALL THIS CARL TO WARN HIM. IF YOU BETRAY ME, OR IF I HEAR THAT YOU HAVE BOUGHT SO MUCH AS HAIR FROM A BARBER-SHOP...
...I WILL BE BACK, AND YOUR WOMAN WILL NEED TO FIND A NEW TOY TO PLAY WITH.

MAN, THAT'S RIDICULOUS! I HAVE TO MAKE A LIVING!

YOU SEE WHAT I DID TO HIS HAND?

IMAGINE WHAT I MIGHT DO TO SOMETHING SOFTER.

MEXICO, 1973.
<YOU'RE CERTAIN IT IS THE JUNKYARD, BUJO?>
<IT DOES SEEM AN APPROPRIATE PLACE FOR A VILLAIN TO MAKE HIS HOME.>
COMIDA REPUGNANTE
CHATARRA
FARMACIA DE LA OFERTA
ALMACEA

<YES, WITH THE REST OF THE TRASH!>
<HA! OH YES! HAHAHAHA VERY GOOD.>

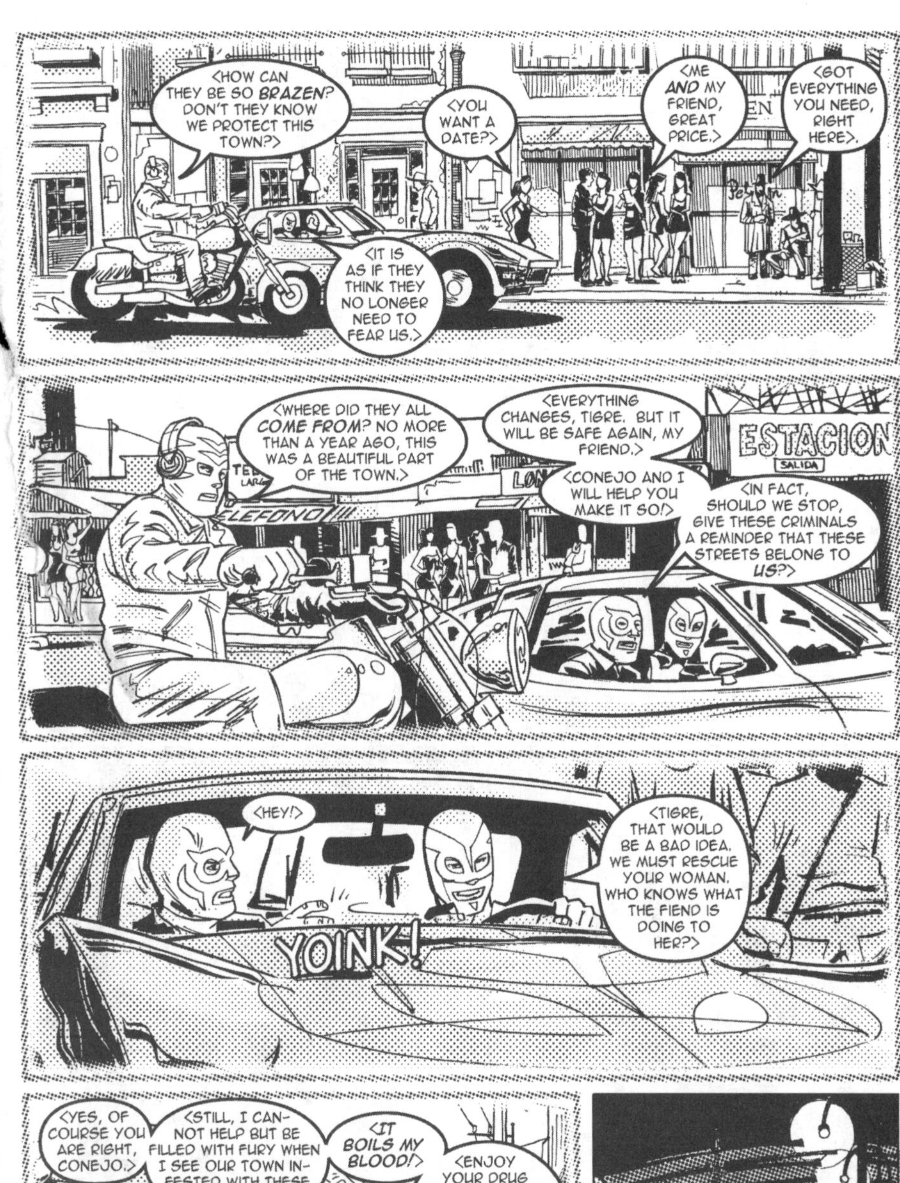
<HOW CAN THEY BE SO **BRAZEN**? DON'T THEY KNOW WE PROTECT THIS TOWN?>
<YOU WANT A DATE?>
<ME **AND** MY FRIEND, GREAT PRICE.>
<GOT EVERYTHING YOU NEED, RIGHT HERE>.
<IT IS AS IF THEY THINK THEY NO LONGER NEED TO FEAR US.>
<WHERE DID THEY ALL *COME FROM*? NO MORE THAN A YEAR AGO, THIS WAS A BEAUTIFUL PART OF THE TOWN.>
<EVERYTHING CHANGES, TIGRE. BUT IT WILL BE SAFE AGAIN, MY FRIEND.>
<CONEJO AND I WILL HELP YOU MAKE IT SO!>
<IN FACT, SHOULD WE STOP, GIVE THESE CRIMINALS A REMINDER THAT THESE STREETS BELONG TO *US*?>
ESTACION
SALIDA
<HEY!>
<TIGRE, THAT WOULD BE A BAD IDEA. WE MUST RESCUE YOUR WOMAN. WHO KNOWS WHAT THE FIEND IS DOING TO HER?>
YOINK!

<YES, OF COURSE YOU ARE RIGHT, CONEJO.>
<STILL, I CAN-NOT HELP BUT BE FILLED WITH FURY WHEN I SEE OUR TOWN IN-FESTED WITH THESE COCKROACHES.>
<IT *BOILS MY BLOOD!*>
<ENJOY YOUR DRUG MONEY WHILE YOU CAN! YOU WILL SEE US AGAIN SOON-ER THAN YOU WOULD LIKE, I THINK!>
CONEJO

MANHATTAN
CENTRAL PARK
TOLL PLAZA AHEAD
CASH ONLY

WAKE UP AMERICA!
TODAY
Jorje Delgado
New York, New York!
NEW WORLD AIRLINES DAILY SERVICE FROM MANCHESTER TO NEW YORK WWW.WORLDAL.CO.UK
THEATER CENTER • • VISIT YOUR L
duane reade
PHARMACY GREETINGS
CLEANERS
HATS GLOVES
OPENS NOVEM
Rays Pizza
YOU HAVE A REST-ROOM?
VOTE JORJE DELGADO
duane

MONTECINO'S PIZZE
SLICES
PIES

SMALL
MED
LARGE
EXIT
OTIS, THAT YOU? WHAT THE HELL HAPPENED TO YOU, MAN?
ACCIDENT.

WELL, I GUESS SO! YOU OK?
I AM FINE. I HAVE YOUR DELIVERY.

ABOUT TIME, TOO. YOU'RE LATE.
LET'S HAVE A LOOK.
CAMPIONATO MONDIALE CALCIO

SWEETMEATS.

WONDERFUL. NICE AND FRESH. TELL LITTLE PEDRO HE DID A GOOD JOB. MY CLIENT WILL BE HAPPY WITH THESE.
YOUR CLIENT?

YEAH, MY CLIENT. WHAT ARE YOU DOING ASKING ABOUT THAT? YOUR ACCIDENT RATTLE YOUR HEAD A LITTLE? YOU KNOW BETTER.
IT PROBABLY DID. MY APOLOGIES.

OKAY, GET THE HELL OUT OF HERE. YOU'RE SCARING THE KIDS. AND TELL LITTLE PEDRO TO BE ON TIME NEXT TIME, GOD-DAMMIT.

JORGE DELGADO
FOR CITY COUNCIL
MONTECINO'S PIZZERIA

MONTECINO'S PIZZERIA

BRAPPP!!

PHPPPPP
VROOOMM!!

MAY I HELP YOU?

I HAVE SENATOR WILLIAMS HERE FOR THE PARTY.
OF COURSE, SIR. JUST A MO- MENT AND WE'LL SEND YOU THROUGH.

WHAM!
WHAM!
WHAM!
WHAM!

HNNH. BIG HOUSE.

FINALLY! I ALMOST HAD TO MAKE A SUB-STITUTION!
QUITE.

JUST GIVE ME THE COOLER, PRICK.

AHH... MARVELOUS.

CHOP!

CHOP
CHOP
CHOP

SIZZLE
SIZZLE

PERFECT.

MADRE DE DIÓS.

AND WHAT DO WE HAVE HERE?
WARM SWEETMEATS AND FENNEL SALAD ON TOAST, SIR.
AHH, AS I THOUGHT.

MY DARLING, YOU SIMPLY MUST TRY ONE OF THESE.
ONE OF MY CHEF'S SPECIAL-TIES. EXQUISITE.

OH MY GOD. THIS IS *INCREDIBLE*.
YES, ISN'T IT?

I ALLOW MY CHEF TO USE ONLY THE *CHOICEST* INGREDIENTS.

THIS SHALL *NOT STAND!*

HEY! YOU THERE! WHAT ARE YOU DOING?
INTRUDER SPOTTED AT THE WEST BALLROOM WINDOW, REQUESTING IMMEDIATE BACKUP!

STOP! STOP RIGHT THERE, OR...

WHOOMP!
NNGHH!

HALT, OR I'LL SHOOT!
I'VE GOT HIM ON THE SECURITY CAM. HE'S HEADED STRAIGHT FOR THE GATE. HE'S---
KONK!
OOF!

CRA ASH!
314 WEST HANCOCK BLVD
314 WEST HANCOCK BLVD

I'M SORRY, SIR, HE MADE IT PAST THE GATES. HE'S GONE.

GOLD DIAMONDS WATCHES
GOLD DIAMONDS WATCHES
Frank's PAPAYA
Frank's PAPAYA
SUBWAY
SUBWAY
JACKSON HEWITT
PHO BANG
PHO BANG

EXCUSE ME, SIR. WAS THERE NOT A FLOWER STAND HERE JUST YESTERDAY?

SHIT, MAN, IF YOU'RE REALLY THERE, THEN I AIN'T GOT NOTHIN' TO GET ROBBED OF. AND IF YOU AIN'T REALLY THERE, THEN, WELL...

... SHIT, MAN.

PLEASE, SIR. FOR YOUR OWN SAKE, GET YOURSELF CLEANED UP.

WRONG CORNER. MUST BE.

KNOCK KNOCK
2:15 AM
UHH... JUST A MINUTE, PLEASE.

TIGRE, DID I WAKE YOU?
DON'T BE SILLY. I AM GLAD YOU ARE HERE. COME IN.
EXIT
PLEASE, SIT.
MAY I OFFER YOU SOMETHING TO DRINK?
I HAVE... THERE'S WATER, AND I CAN MAKE COFFEE.
WHISKEY, IF YOU PREFER.
YOU MUST FORGIVE ME. I HAVE NOTHING ELSE TO OFFER.
IT HAS BEEN SO LONG SINCE I HAVE HAD GUESTS.
NO, NO, I AM FINE. PLEASE, DON'T APOLOGIZE!
YOU SEEM SURPRISED TO SEE ME.
IN FACT, I WAS JUST LOOKING FOR YOU AT YOUR FLOWER BOOTH, BUT...
I WAS NOT THERE! OF COURSE NOT! WHO HAS NEED FOR A BLOSSOM SO LATE?
YES, OF COURSE. BUT IT WASN'T JUST THAT IT WAS CLOSED. THE BOOTH ITSELF...
TIGRE, HAVE YOU LEARNED ANYTHING YET?
I DO NOT WISH TO RUSH YOU, BUT I AM SO AFRAID SOME-THING TERRIBLE IS GOING ON.
NOT AT ALL. LITTLE MARIA, I AM ALMOST AFRAID TO TELL YOU WHAT I SAW TONIGHT.
DO NOT SPARE ME THE TRUTH. IGNORING EVIL IS THE SUREST WAY TO LET IT PROSPER.

WELL SAID.
MARIA...

THE FLESH OUR PEOPLE SELL. IT IS BEING CONSUMED...

...AS FOOD.
CHRIST IN HEAVEN!
WHO IS DOING THIS?

I DO NOT KNOW... YET. BUT I FOLLOWED THE TRAIL TO A MANSION OUTSIDE OF TOWN. I HAD TO LEAVE BEFORE I DETERMINED THE TRUTH BEHIND THIS HORROR, BUT I HAVE THE ADDRESS. I WILL DISCOVER WHO OWNS THE MANSION.

AND WHAT WILL YOU DO THEN?
I WILL LEARN HOW DEEP THE PLOT GOES. THESE WERE RICH, POWERFUL PEOPLE, MARIA. IT WILL NOT BE EASY TO GO AGAINST THEM. BUT I WILL GO.
AND THEN EVERY PERSON WHO KNOWINGLY ATE THE FLESH OF OUR COUNTRY-MEN WILL PAY.

THIS WILL *NOT* STAND.
I KNEW YOU WOULD HELP US. I *KNEW* IT!

IT IS NOTHING. IT IS AS YOU SAID. THIS IS WHAT I AM SUPPOSED TO BE DOING. I MUST THANK YOU, MARIA. THIS WORK YOU ASKED ME TO DO-
IT HAS BROUGHT ME BACK TO *LIFE*. MY HEART BEATS AGAIN, MY ARMS HAVE REGAINED THEIR STRENGTH.

ALLOW ME TO APOLOGIZE. I SHOULD NEVER HAVE TAKEN YOUR MONEY.
NO, IT IS YOURS. PLEASE, IF IT CAN HELP IN ANY WAY, TAKE IT.
MARIA, YOU ARE GENEROUS, AND KIND, BUT THIS IS NOW A MATTER OF HONOR. I CANNOT ACCEPT MONEY FOR IT.
MARIA...
SHHH.

DO YOU ALWAYS WEAR THIS?
ALWAYS.
THE OLD HEROES NEVER REMOVED THEIR MASKS, EVEN WITH EACH OTHER. IT WAS OUR RULE. WE HAD TO BE SYMBOLS OF GOODNESS, OF STRENGTH. WITHOUT THE MASKS, WE WERE ONLY MEN.

I UNDER-STAND.
BUT TONIGHT, I DO NOT NEED THE SYMBOL...

...I NEED THE MAN.

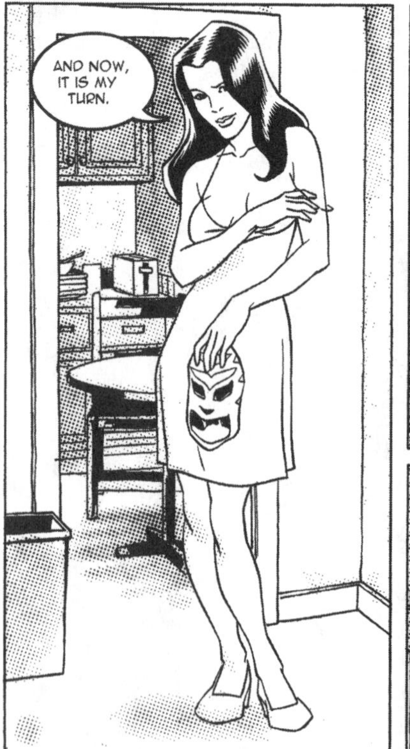
AND NOW, IT IS MY TURN.

HOW?
MARIA?
NNNGH!
RAAAARGHHHHH!!!

YOU DON'T NEED THE MASK. DOCTOR-PATIENT CONFIDENTIALITY.
IT IS NOT MY HEAD THAT IS INJURED. THE MASK REMAINS.
TRYING TO MAKE SURE I CAN'T TELL THE COPS WHO YOU ARE? LOOK, ALL I CARE ABOUT IS MAKING PEOPLE WELL.
HOW YOU GOT THIS WAY IS YOUR BUSINESS.
BUT I TOLD YOU, I DID NOT...
YEAH, YEAH. YOU THINK YOU'RE THE FIRST PERSON TO COME IN HERE SHY A KIDNEY OR SOME-THING AND SAY THEY FELL DOWN THE STAIRS?
IT IS THE TRUTH. A WOMAN I TRUSTED USED ME... POORLY. SHE SEDUCED ME AND STOLE MY KIDNEY TO SELL IT.
KIDNEY? YOU AREN'T MISSING A KIDNEY.
BUT YOU JUST SAID...
NOPE, I DIDN'T. YOU STILL HAVE BOTH KIDNEYS, FOR WHAT THAT'S WORTH.
NO, FOR SOME INSANE REASON, YOU SEEM TO HAVE SOLD HALF YOUR LIVER.
MY... LIVER?
YES, AND WHO KNOWS WHY? IF THE HALF YOU SOLD IS IN ANYTHING LIKE THE CONDITION OF WHAT'S LEFT,
I WOULDN'T HAVE GIVEN YOU MORE THAN OH, MAYBE THREE BUCKS AND CHANGE FOR IT.
I DO NOT UNDERSTAND. SPEAK PLAINLY.

MY PLEASURE. AFTER THE WAY YOU'VE OBVIOUSLY BEEN TREATING YOUR LIVER FOR THE PAST TWENTY YEARS,
YOU WERE BARELY SURVIVING ON A WHOLE ONE.
WITH HALF, YOU'VE GOT A COUPLE OF WEEKS, TOPS, UNLESS YOU GET A TRANSPLANT.
NO.
YES. AND SO YOU SEE WHY IT'S SO HARD FOR ME TO UNDERSTAND? YOU THREW YOUR LIFE AWAY FOR WHAT, A FEW WEEKS' BEER MONEY?
WHERE THE HELL DO YOU THINK YOU'RE GOING? I'M TRANSFERRING YOU TO ST. BART'S.
MY CLOTHES.
THEY'LL PUT YOU ON THE TRANSPLANT LIST.
LIKE HELL. PERHAPS I DIDN'T MAKE MYSELF CLEAR. YOU'RE DYING. I'M TRYING TO HELP YOU. THERE'S STILL A CHANCE.
MY CLOTHES.
CHRIST, YOU'RE ACTUALLY REFUSING TO GIVE ME INFORMED CONSENT. WHAT'S THE POINT? WHY'D I EVEN BOTHER?
YOU WANT TO GET OUT OF HERE? FINE.
PAINKILLERS, AND ANTIBIOTICS. ONE OF EACH, MORNING AND EVENING. MIGHT AS WELL AVOID A STAPH INFECTION, RIGHT?
HAVE FUN FINISHING THE JOB OF KILLING YOURSELF. NEXT TIME SAVE ME THE TROUBLE AND JUMP OFF A ROOF.
THANK YOU FOR EVERYTHING. DESPITE WHAT YOU THINK, YOUR WORK IS NOT WASTED.
WHATEVER MAKES YOU HAPPY, DEAD MAN.

DING!
L 1
2 3
4 5
6 7
8 9

JORGE DELGADO
FOR CITY COUNCIL

...ONLY THE *CHOICEST* INGREDIENTS.

VINTNER
CAMPAIGN

NO PARKING
STORAGE
BICKLE'S PICKLES
YOU TALKIN' TO ME?
TAKE OUT
REPAIR
DELGADO FOR CITY COUNCIL
JORGE DELGADO
FOR CITY COUNCIL

N. VINTNER ST
EXCUSE ME, CAN I HELP YOU?
THIS IS THE OFFICE OF JORGE DELGADO, YES?
WHY YES, BUT WHAT DOES THAT HAVE TO DO WITH SOMEONE LIKE YOU?

SOMEONE LIKE ME HAS TAKEN A STRONG INTEREST IN MR. DELGADO'S CAMPAIGN. SOMEONE LIKE ME NEEDS TO SEE HIM IMMEDIATELY.

I SEE. WELL, OF COURSE WE APPRECIATE YOUR SUPPORT. WHY DON'T YOU TELL ME ABOUT YOUR GRAVE MATTER, AND WE'LL SEE IF WE CAN'T GET YOU AN APPOINTMENT SOME TIME IN THE FUTURE. OF COURSE, YOU REALIZE HOW BUSY MR. DELGADO IS, AND...

I HAVE NO TIME FOR YOU.
JORGE DELGADO
HUNGRY FOR CHANGE!

FOR CITY COUNCIL
SHAWN! LUIS! THIS MAN ATTACKED ME! I THINK HE'S GOING TO HURT MR. DELGADO!

CITY COUNCIL
JORGE DELGADO
HUNGRY

NOW, I WAS WATCHING WHAT HAPPENED, SIR, AND I KNOW YOU DIDN'T ATTACK ANYONE,
BUT YOU CAN'T JUST COME BARGING AROUND BACK HERE.
I MUST SPEAK TO DELGADO.
NOT GOING TO HAPPEN, BIG GUY.

BOTH OF YOU, STEP ASIDE.
THAT'S NOT GOING TO HAPPEN, EITHER.
JORGE DELGADO
HUNGRY
JUST GET ON WITH IT!
CALM DOWN, LUIS.

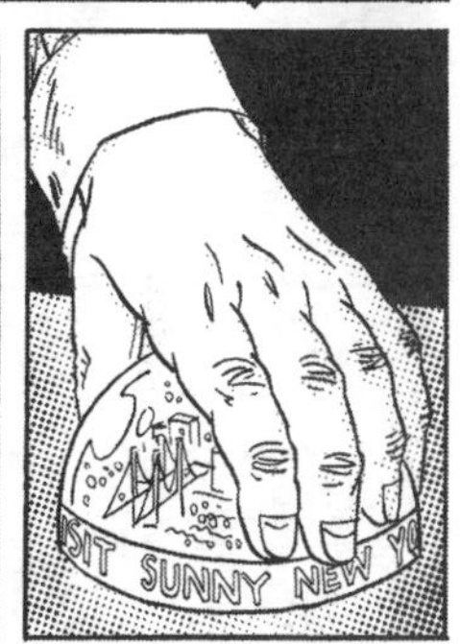
SIT SUNNY NEW YO

KRAK!
AAAGH!

COWARD.

CRASH!

YES. THAT IS THE WAY IT SHOULD BE DONE.

POW!

KROM!

YOU AGAIN!
HAVE YOU
LEARNED
NOTHING?

RING-RING!

YES, MR. DEL-
GADO? NO, NO,
NOTHING TO
WORRY ABOUT
UP FRONT.

WHAT?
ARE YOU
SURE?
YES, I
HEARD
YOU,
BUT...
YES,
SIR. OF
COURSE,
SIR. RIGHT
AWAY.

LET HIM
UP.
EXCUSE
ME??
YOU
HEARD ME!
LET HIM
UP.
MR. DELGADO
WANTS TO SEE
HIM IMMED-
IATELY. ALONE.

JORGE
DELGAD

PLEASE, HAVE A SEAT.
NOW, I AM GOING TO PUT THIS GUN DOWN, AND WE SHALL HAVE A CHAT.
BUT THIS IS *MY* OFFICE, AND *YOU* ARE THE MASKED MAN WHO DOES NOT BELONG HERE.
IF YOU ATTEMPT TO HARM ME, NO ONE WOULD QUESTION ME IF I SHOT YOU.
SO PLEASE, DON'T MAKE ME SHOOT YOU.
AGREED?
AGREED.
GOOD. NOW, I AM JORGE DELGADO. AND WHO ARE YOU?
I AM CALLED *TIGRE*.

A STRONG NAME. IT SUITS YOU.
SO, *TIGRE*, WHAT CAN I DO FOR YOU?

YOU CAN STOP EATING THE FLESH OF YOUR COUNTRY-MEN.

YOU CAN RELEASE MY FRIEND, WHO I AM SORRY I SUSPECTED OF ANY WRONG.

YOU CAN RETURN TO ME THE HALF OF MY LIVER YOU STOLE.

AND THEN YOU CAN REPENT IN SOLITUDE FOR THE REST OF YOUR DAYS, IN HOPES THAT YOUR SOUL MIGHT SPEND A FEW LESS HOURS IN ***HELL***.

IS THAT ALL?

IF A SINGLE MAN WERE TRULY RESPONSIBLE FOR ALL THAT, HE'D BE SOME SORT OF DEVIL!
NO ONE IS THAT BAD, MY FRIEND!
SO YOU DENY IT?
OF COURSE I DENY IT!
YOU WALK INTO MY OFFICE AND ACCUSE ME OF BEING AN ORGAN-STEALING, KIDNAPPING CANNIBAL.
WHAT DO YOU EXPECT ME TO SAY?
BUT THE EVIDENCE IS HERE! YOU ARE A KIDNAPPER. YOU CANNOT ARGUE WITH THIS.
AND YET I DO.
NOW, SEÑOR TIGRE, I AM SYMPATHETIC TO THE PLIGHT OF THE MENTALLY ILL. I HAVE DONATED A GREAT DEAL OF MONEY TO HELP POOR LUNATICS SUCH AS YOURSELF.
BUT IT IS TIME FOR YOU TO GO.
DID YOU JUST CALL ME A LUNATIC?
DOES THAT LOOK LIKE THE WORK OF A SANE PERSON?
THE TRUTH IS, TIGRE, YOU'RE JUST A CRAZY OLD MAN WITH DELUSIONS THAT HE WAS ONCE SOMETHING ELSE.
CLICK!
THE TRUTH IS, YOU COULDN'T HAVE BEEN MUCH TO BEGIN WITH, TO END UP LIKE THIS.
THE TRUTH?

THIS IS THE TRUTH!
CRASH!

MR. DELGADO, ARE YOU ALL...
MY GOD!

BOYS!

AGGGGGGGH!!

POLICE, BOSS?
NO. HE'S NO THREAT. JUST DUMP HIM.

DAMN, HE'S HEAVY.

GOOD RIDDANCE, OLD MAN.

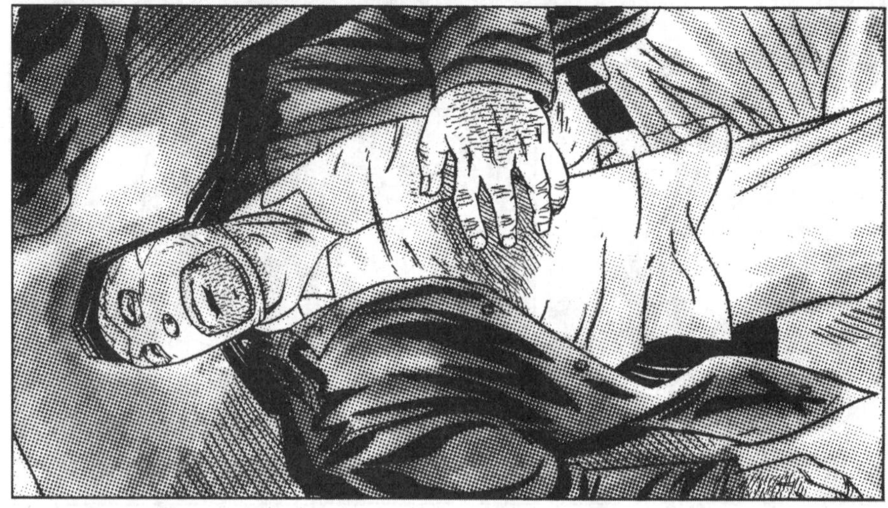

TSK.

ME, A KIDNAPPER? PREPOSTEROUS.

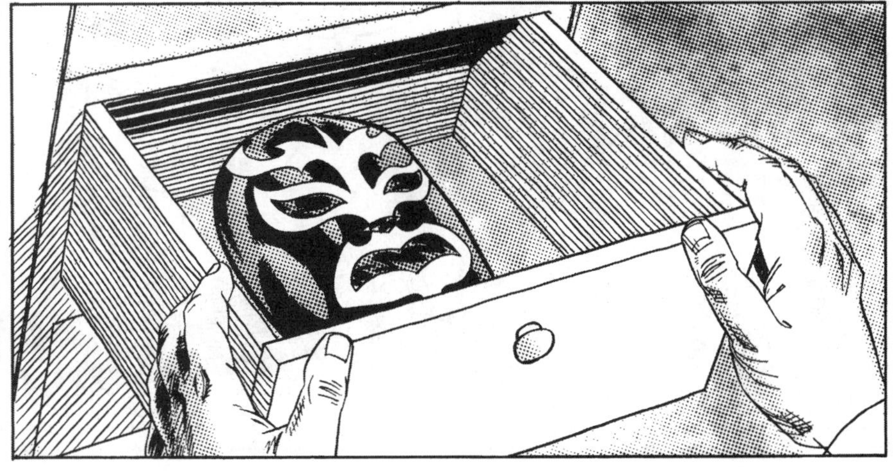

MEXICO, 1973

<THE POWER IF YOU PLEASE, CONEJO.>

<I COUNT TWENTY-FIVE. MOST AT THE GATE. TEN THERE.>
<THEN WE ONLY HAVE TWENTY-FOUR TO DEAL WITH, AS ONE IS MY...>
<THAT'S ASSUMING SHE'S STILL ALIVE. BEST TO PLAN FOR TWENTY-FIVE.>

<TWENTY-FOUR.>

...
<EIGHT EACH, THEN.>

<WE HAVE FACED WORSE ODDS.>
<SO. HOW DO WE GO IN, *BOSS*?>

<WE'LL LET YOU HANDLE THAT.>

NINGUNA VIOLACIO
¡NO HAY PASO!

AY?
POK
FSSSH!
<WHAT THE?>
<THAT'S NO GOOD.>
<STAY ALERT.>
SÍ. <ALWAYS.>
KLONK!
<WHERE ARE THEY???>
EH?
TAP TAP
TAP TAP
<OVER HERE, DUMMY.>
OOF!

GLUURGH!!

<YOU DID NOT NEED TO KILL HIM.>

<RIGHT. SINCERE APOLOGIES, BOSS.>

<QUICKLY. WE MUST GET TO THE CENTER, BEFORE THE OTHER GUARDS COME.>
<THE CENTER? WHY?>

<WHERE ELSE TO KEEP THE PRINCESS, BUT THE CENTER OF THE MAZE?>

NINGUNA VIOLACION ¡NO HAY PASO!

<MY LOVE! WHAT HAVE THEY DONE TO HER?>
<DO NOT BE AFRAID, MY DARLING.>

<BUJO! CONEJO! HELP ME!>

<I AM COMING!>
PAT Rc 27

AGH!!
BLAM!

<TIGRE, I CAN'T MOVE. MY... I THINK IT'S MY SPINE.>
<DON'T MOVE, OLD FRIEND.
CONEJO! I NEED YOU! CONE--

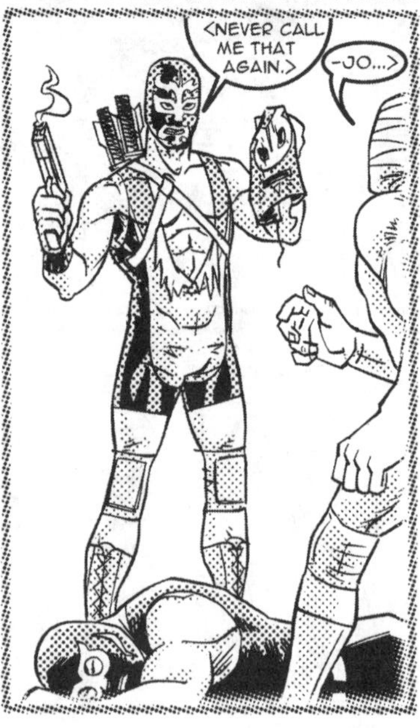
<NEVER CALL ME THAT AGAIN.>
-JO...>

<WHY???>
<WHY DID I DO THIS, TIGRE? BETTER TO ASK WHY I DIDN'T DO IT EARLIER.>
<YOU THINK I LIKE BEING YOUR APPRENTICE?>
<DOING WHAT YOU AND THE OLD MAN TELL ME TO DO?>
<YOU LITTLE...>
<NO, NO, YOU STAY WHERE YOU ARE.>
KPOW!
KPOW!
KPOW!
SPANG!
SPANG!
SPANG!
<BUT HOW COULD YOU HAVE BECOME THIS MONSTER?>
<WE TRAINED YOU TO BE A HERO, NOT...>
<ENOUGH. I DID NOT BRING YOU HERE TO EXPLAIN MYSELF.>
<I BROUGHT YOU HERE TO BE RID OF YOU.>
<THINGS ARE CHANGING IN MEXICO, TIGRE.>
<I INTEND TO BE PART OF IT, IN A WAY YOU COULD NEVER BE. YOU WOULDN'T KNOW HOW TO BEGIN.
<ALL ALONG, IT HAS BEEN YOU, BRINGING THE CRIME INTO THE TOWN.>
<A MAN HAS A RIGHT TO MAKE A LIVING, YES?>
<NOW, I SHALL LEAVE YOU SHORTLY, AND WHEN I DO, I SHALL LEAVE MY MASK BEHIND FOREVER. BUT YOU SEE THE PROBLEM?>
<YOU HAVE NEVER SEEN MY FACE.>
<YOUR RULE, OF COURSE. "WE MUST ALWAYS BE MASKED, TO REMAIN ICONS TO THE PEOPLE.">
<IF YOU KNEW MY TRUE FACE, YOU MIGHT SOMEDAY SEEK YOUR REVENGE. BUT AS IT IS, I WILL REMAIN A MYSTERY TO YOU.>
<BUT THAT IS FITTING.>
<I ALWAYS WAS.>

<THERE IS ONE THING I HAVE ALWAYS WONDERED, TIGRE. JUST HOW STRONG *ARE* YOU?>

THRUMMMM
SCREEECH!
VROOM!
<CHRIST ON THE CROSS!>
<SHALL WE FIND OUT?>

NNNGH!
KPOW! KPOW!

<GOOD-BYE, MY FRIENDS, AND GOOD LUCK!>

RRRRRNH!

SKKKTCH..

<NO!>

27,194
CAUTION HIGH VOLTAGE
<NO!!>
<I. WILL. NOT. LET. YOU. DIE!!!>
<YES!!>
BANG!
AAAH!
!
<STRONGER THAN I WOULD HAVE GUESSED. IMPRESSIVE.>
27,194
...MARIA....

<TIGRE! MY FRIEND! THIS IS A WELCOME SURPRISE.>

<GOOD EVENING, BUJO.>
<WHAT HAPPENED TO YOU?>
<ARE YOU ALL RIGHT?>

<NO.>
<I AM DYING.>

<HA! THE IDEA THAT I WOULD OUTLIVE YOU? IMPOSSIBLE.>
<BUT IT IS TRUE. I HAVE BEEN STUPID, AND NOW I PAY THE PRICE.>

<MARIA CAME TO ME, JUST AS SHE USED TO, AND ASKED ME FOR HELP. I TRIED TO SAY NO TO HER, I TRIED, BUT THE WAY SHE SPOKE... SHE MADE ME FORGET EVERY-THING THAT HAP-PENED TO US.>

<I REMEMBERED MY STRENGTH, BUJO! FOR A TIME, IT WAS GLORIOUS.>
<OH, TIGRE, TIGRE.>
<THERE IS A MAN - HIS NAME IS DELGADO. HE IS EVIL, BUJO. HE STOLE MY VERY FLESH, AND KIDNAPPED MARIA! I TRIED TO STOP HIM, BUT I WAS TOO WEAK.>

<MY FRIEND, MARIA IS DEAD. SHE DIED THAT DAY IN THE JUNKYARD, THIRTY YEARS AGO.>

<I KNOW THAT.>
<OF COURSE I KNOW THAT. BUT SHE RETURNED TO ME.>

....
<I SUPPOSE THE WORLD IS A STRANGE PLACE. WE FOUGHT VAMPIRE WOMEN, ALIENS FROM SPACE...>
<WHY IS IT IMPOSSIBLE THAT YOUR LOVE COULD RETURN TO YOU?>

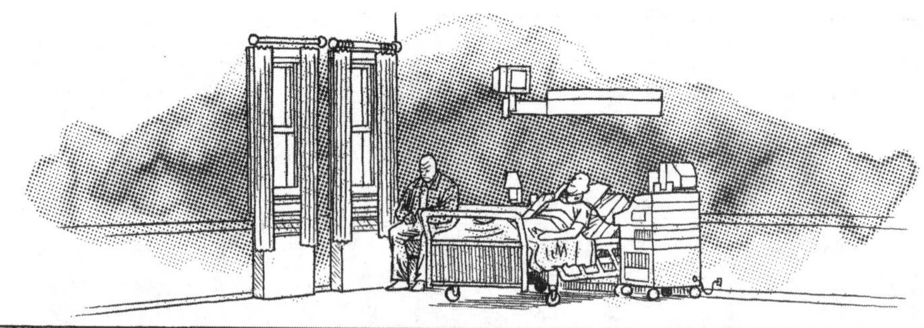

<BUT DID WE REALLY FIGHT MONSTERS, BUJO? WAS ANY OF IT REAL? I SEE THE FILMS ON THE TELEVISION, AND THAT OLD LIFE FEELS LIKE A DREAM. IT WAS ALL SO CLEAR BACK THEN, UNTIL...>

EL DIABLO AZUL.

CONEJO.

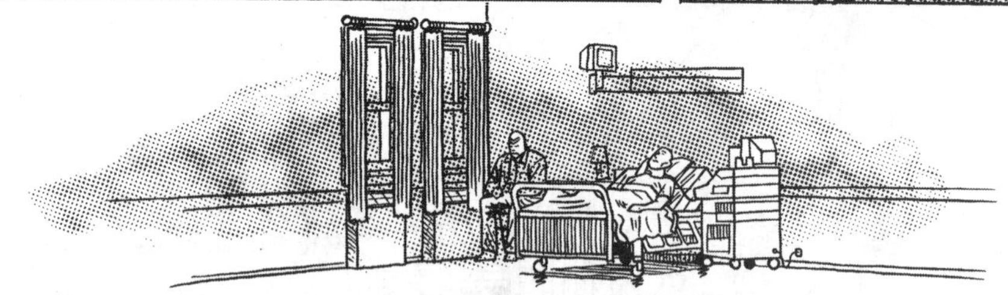

<BUT ENOUGH ABOUT THE PAST. IT'S SO BORING I WOULD GET UP AND WALK AWAY, IF MY LEGS WERE NOT USE-LESS STICKS. WHAT IS THIS YOU SAID ABOUT DYING?>

<UGLY, BUT YOU HAVE BEEN WOUNDED BEFORE AND RECOVERED.>

<IT IS MORE THAN JUST A WOUND. THE TRUE DAMAGE IS INSIDE.>
<HOW LONG?>
<DAYS.>

<THEN WHAT ARE YOU DOING IN A HOSPITAL? BEING STUCK HERE IS MY CURSE, NOT YOURS.>
<YOU SAY THIS MAN DELGADO IS EVIL? TRULY EVIL?>

<AN EVIL A MAN AS I HAVE EVER FACED. HE PREYS UPON HIS PEOPLE, BUJO - OUR PEOPLE. HE IS A LIAR, A THIEF, A KILLER AND A CANNIBAL. AND HE IS RUNNING FOR POLITICAL OFFICE! SOMEONE MUST STOP HIM. I THOUGHT IT COULD BE ME, BUT I WAS A FOOL.>

<TIGRE! YOU WERE NOT FOOLISH TO GO UP AGAINST THIS MAN. YOU ARE BEING FOOLISH NOW.>
<WHAT IS LIFE FOR, TIGRE? IS IT FOR DYING?>
<OF COURSE NOT.>
<OF COURSE NOT. IT IS FOR LIVING. AND FOR MEN LIKE US, LIVING IS ABOUT ONE THING: THE FIGHTING OF EVIL. YOU HAVE FORGOTTEN THAT. WHAT HAPPENED THIRTY YEARS AGO MADE YOU ABANDON WHO YOU ARE, MADE YOU ABANDON YOUR HOMELAND TO COME TO THIS FILTHY, DARK, CROWDED CITY.>

<IF I HAVE FORGOTTEN, IT IS BECAUSE MY FAILURES FILL MY MIND. I FAILED MARIA, I FAILED YOU, AND I FAILED CONEJO. I COULD NOT STAND TO LIVE IN THE SHADOW OF SUCH SHAME. AT LEAST HERE, NO ONE KNOWS WHO I ONCE WAS.>
<PERHAPS. BUT THIRTY YEARS IS TIME ENOUGH TO ATONE FOR MANY SINS. IF YOU HAVE ONLY DAYS LEFT, USE THEM TO DO WHAT YOU WERE BORN TO DO.>
<YOU ARE WHAT YOU ARE, MY FRIEND - A HERO FOR THE PEOPLE. WHAT GREATER REASON DO YOU NEED TO ACT? STOPPING MEN LIKE DELGADO IS WHY YOU EXIST.>
<BUT HOW? I AM IN AGONY EVEN AS I SIT HERE.>

<AHH, NOW. I THINK I MAY BE ABLE TO HELP YOU WITH THAT. OPEN THE TOP DRAWER OF THE TABLE HERE, AT THE BEDSIDE.>
<WHAT IS THIS?>
<OPEN IT. MIX A QUANTITY WITH WATER AND DRINK IT.>
<WHAT *IS* IT?>
<SOMETHING I DEVELOPED FROM PLANTS AND HERBS BACK HOME. I USE IT WHEN THE PAIN IS TOO TERRIBLE. DRINK IT.>
<DELICIOUS, NO?>
<THE... THE PAIN!>
<GONE. ORDINARILY, I WOULD SAY TO BE CAUTIOUS, BECAUSE WHEN THERE IS NO PAIN YOU ARE MORE LIKELY TO INJURE YOURSELF WITHOUT REALIZING IT. BUT YOU ARE LUCKY - AS YOU ARE DYING ANYWAY, IT DOES NOT MATTER!>

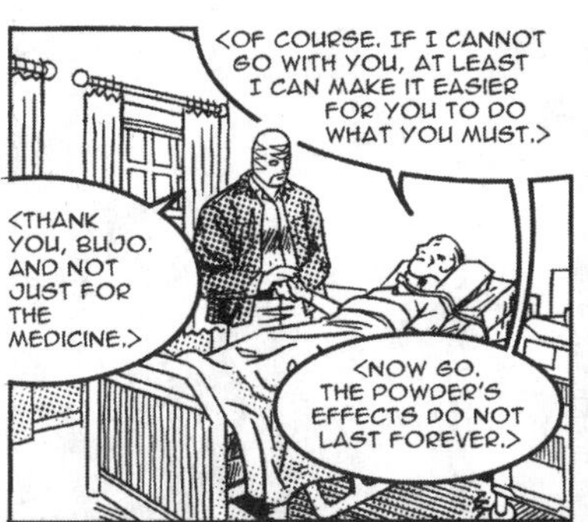
<OF COURSE. IF I CANNOT GO WITH YOU, AT LEAST I CAN MAKE IT EASIER FOR YOU TO DO WHAT YOU MUST.>
<THANK YOU, BUJO. AND NOT JUST FOR THE MEDICINE.>
<NOW GO. THE POWDER'S EFFECTS DO NOT LAST FOREVER.>

<I WILL DIE BY *LIVING*. IT IS THE BEST WAY.>

<CERTAINLY. BUT BEFORE YOU DO, CHANGE YOUR CLOTHES, AND TAKE A SHOWER.>
<HEROES SHOULD NOT LOOK LIKE FILTHY HOBOS.>

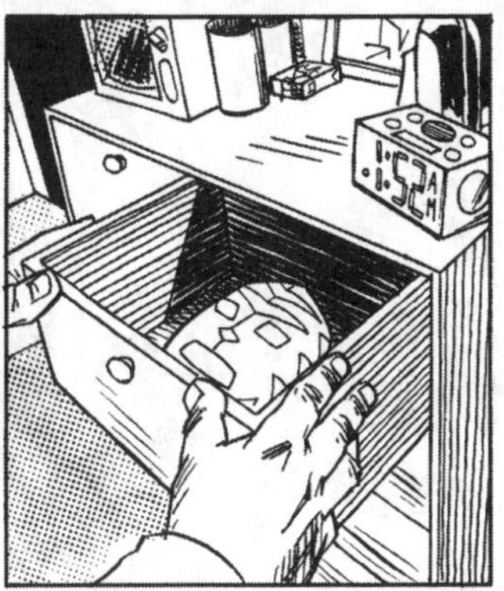

JARRITOS
GUAYABA

BA-DOOM!
HOLY CHRIST!

HEY, YOU SEE THAT? WHAT THE HELL IS THAT?

GET UP TO THE HOUSE, QUICK! SEE IF THEY HAVE FIRE EXTINGUISHERS! I'LL OPEN THE GATES!
RRUMBLE!
WHAT THE HELL?
VROOOM!
VROOOOM!
AAH!
SHI--!
BOOM!
SECURITY ALERT! ONE MAN, VERY, VERY HOSTILE. HE'S HEADED FOR THE FRONT DOOR!

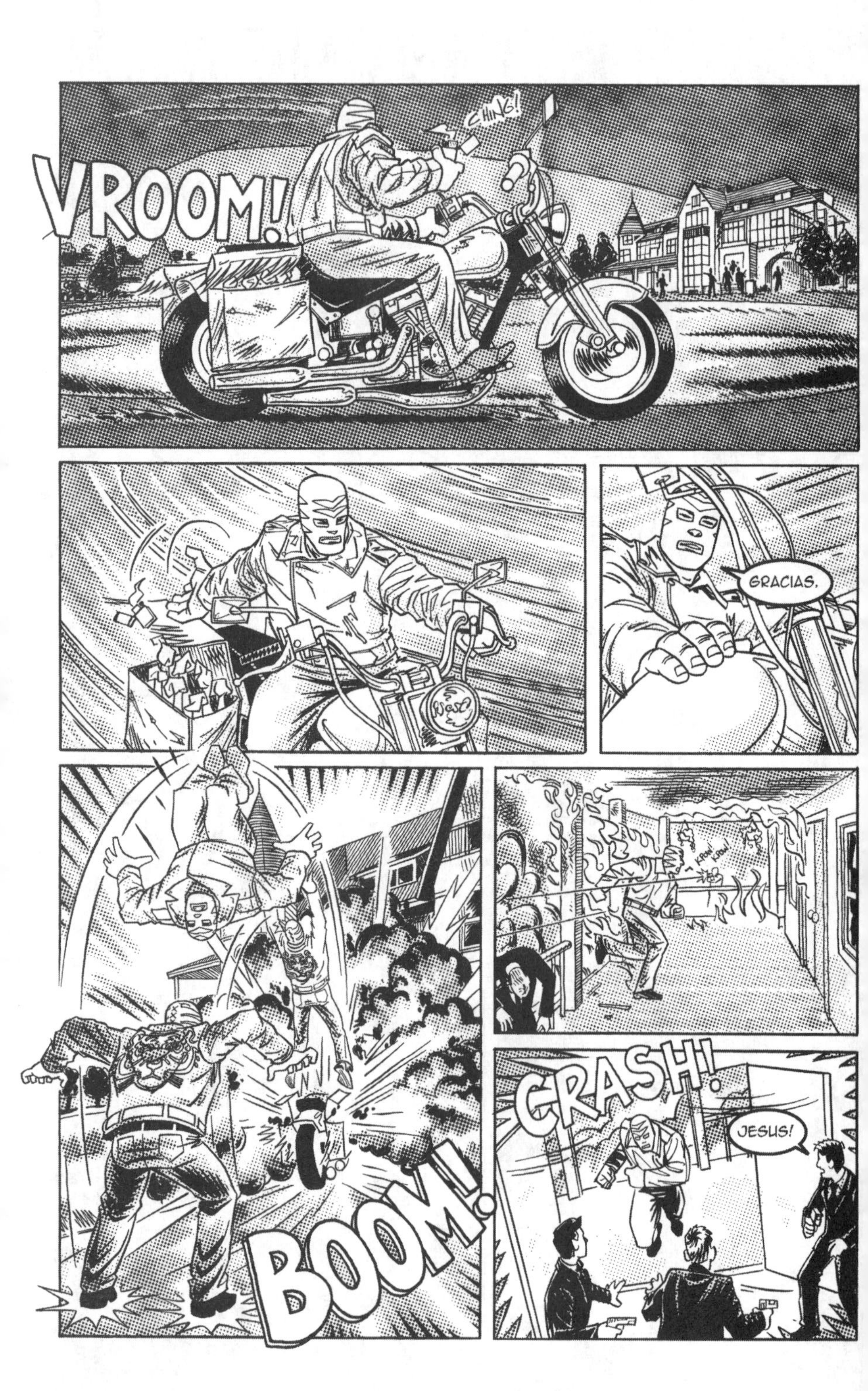
VROOM!
CHING!
GRACIAS.
BOOM!
KPOW!
KPOW!
CRASH!
JESUS!

DELGADO!!
U-UP-STAIRS!
THUNK!
OOF!
OOPS.
PAT PAT
K-POW!
WHAP!

K-POW!
SPANG!

THUD!
KPOW!
KPOW!
SPANG! SPANG!

SHOVE!

THANK YOU, TIGRE. THIS WAY WE WILL REMAIN UNDISTURBED.

I HAVE COME FOR YOU.
YES, YES, I KNOW. WE WILL GET TO THAT. BUT FIRST, PLEASE, JOIN ME.

WOULD YOU CARE FOR SOME PATE? IT'S QUITE SPECIAL, VERY DIFFI-CULT TO OBTAIN. I MYSELF HAVE NEVER TRIED IT BEFORE. I AM QUITE LOOKING FORWARD TO A TASTE.
YOU ARE INSANE!

NO? MORE FOR ME, THEN.

EEEEUCH!

TO BE EXPECTED, I SUPPOSE. SOMEONE SPENT A GOOD WHILE PICKLING THIS PAR-TICULAR LIVER. AH WELL. SHALL WE GET TO THE MAIN DISH?

MONSTER!

WELL, CERTAINLY. YOU CAN STOP RIGHT THERE, HOWEVER.
I HAVE SOMETHING TO SHOW YOU.

DRAMATIC TELEVISION FOOTAGE IN SITUATIONS LIKE THIS...
....MY ONE GREAT WEAK-NESS.

WHERE IS SHE?
OH, QUITE CLOSE.
COME, I WILL TAKE YOU TO HER.
BUT FIRST...

BANG! BANG! BANG! BANG!

...DON'T GET ANY IDEAS.

AFTER YOU, SEÑOR TIGRE.

HAVE YOU COME TO UNDER-STAND? YOU KNOW WHO I AM?
....
EL DIABLO AZUL.

AH, GOOD. I THOUGHT I MIGHT HAVE TO PULL OUT MY OLD MASK IF YOU DIDN'T SEE IT SOON.
I DIDN'T WANT TO - VILLAINS THESE DAYS HAVE NO NEED FOR MASKS. THE WORLD ENJOYS ITS VILLAINS.
IT'S THE HEROES WHO MUST HIDE THEIR FACES. THEY DON'T FIT, YOU SEE.
ANYONE WHO TRIES TO HELP IN THIS WORLD COMES OFF AS, WELL... CRAZY.
WHY?
STILL YOUR FAVORITE QUESTION, I SEE.
SO. WHY DID I ENGINEER A BANQUET AT WHICH OUR PEOPLE WERE FED TO MY WEALTHIEST POLITICAL BACKERS? WELL, TIGRE, IT WAS AMUSING.
FILLING THE BELLIES OF THIS CITY'S RICH AND POWERFUL WITH THE FLESH OF THE POOR HAD A LOVELY SYMMETRY I COULD NOT PASS UP.
IT ALREADY HAPPENS IN EVERY SENSE BUT THE MOST LITERAL - I SIMPLY TOOK IT UPON MYSELF TO TAKE THAT FINAL STEP ON THEIR BEHALF.
STILL, I THINK MY CANNIBAL PHASE IS OVER. IT WAS A GOOD JOKE WHILE IT LASTED, BUT IT'S TIME FOR SOMETHING NEW.

OH, I'M SORRY, THAT WASN'T THE ANSWER YOU WANTED? LET'S SEE. WHY DID I BETRAY YOU THIRTY YEARS AGO?
WHY??
BECAUSE, TIGRE, A LIFE FILLED WITH FIGHTING THE GOOD FIGHT, TURNING DOWN REWARDS, LISTENING TO YOU AND OLD BUJO NATTERING ON ABOUT MY TRAINING WHEN I WAS ALWAYS TWICE THE FIGHTER OF BOTH OF YOU COMBINED...
WELL, IT SEEMED LIKE IT MIGHT NOT HOLD MY INTEREST IN THE LONG RUN.
WHAT I WANTED WAS A LIFE WITH NO RESTRICTIONS, NO BOUNDARIES. AND I TOOK IT.

NOW TURN AROUND AND KEEP WALKING, OLD FRIEND.

WHAT IS THIS? WHERE IS MARIA?
GET IN, AND I'LL TELL YOU.

REALLY. WHAT IS THIS?
MARIA IS TIED TO THE BOTTOM OF THIS ELE-VATOR.

SO, GROUND FLOOR, THEN?
3 4
1 2
G
TING!

BASTARD!

TING!
TING!
TING!
TING!
3
1 2
G

WE ARE NOT YET DONE, YOU AND I.

OH, I HOPE NOT.

4
KRAK!
B

NNNNNNGH!
IT IS ALL RIGHT, MARIA! DO NOT BE AFRAID!
OOF!
RRRRRRRGH!

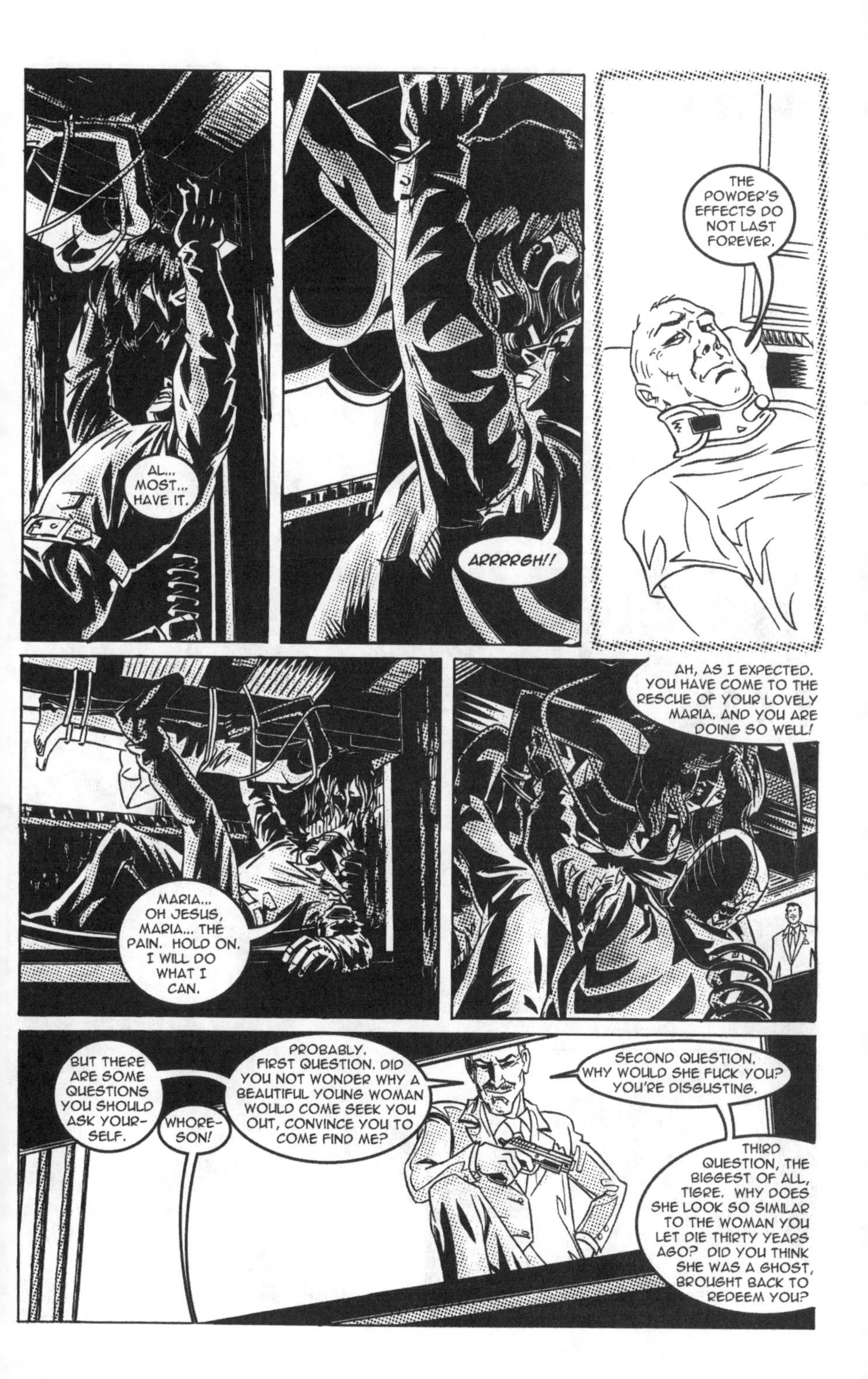
AL... MOST... HAVE IT.
ARRRRGH!!
THE POWDER'S EFFECTS DO NOT LAST FOREVER.
MARIA... OH JESUS, MARIA... THE PAIN. HOLD ON. I WILL DO WHAT I CAN.
AH, AS I EXPECTED. YOU HAVE COME TO THE RESCUE OF YOUR LOVELY MARIA. AND YOU ARE DOING SO WELL!
BUT THERE ARE SOME QUESTIONS YOU SHOULD ASK YOURSELF.
WHORESON!
PROBABLY. FIRST QUESTION. DID YOU NOT WONDER WHY A BEAUTIFUL YOUNG WOMAN WOULD COME SEEK YOU OUT, CONVINCE YOU TO COME FIND ME?
SECOND QUESTION. WHY WOULD SHE FUCK YOU? YOU'RE DISGUSTING.
THIRD QUESTION, THE BIGGEST OF ALL, TIGRE. WHY DOES SHE LOOK SO SIMILAR TO THE WOMAN YOU LET DIE THIRTY YEARS AGO? DID YOU THINK SHE WAS A GHOST, BROUGHT BACK TO REDEEM YOU?

QUIETE!
SUDDENLY YOU'RE SICK OF QUESTIONS? NO, NO, TOO LATE FOR THAT.
HERE IS SOMETHING FUNNY - ALL OF THOSE QUESTIONS HAVE THE SAME ANSWER.
I HIRED HER, TIGRE. SHE IS AN ACTRESS. I PAID HER TO SET YOU ON THE PATH TO ME.
AND JUST SO YOU KNOW, IT COST EXTRA TO GET HER INTO YOUR BED.
MARIA IS AN EXPENSIVE YOUNG WHORE. SHE HAS *BIG DREAMS*, YOU SEE.

LIAR!!!
LOOK AT HER, TIGRE, AND TELL ME IF I'M LYING.

OH, YOU LOOK VERY SAD, TIGRE, VERY SAD INDEED.
BUT I AM GLAD YOU ARE SO DEEPLYAFFECTED. I WENT TO A GREAT DEAL OF EFFORT TO PUT ALL OF THIS TOGETHER.
AND IT'S WORKING, ISN'T IT?
IT'S JUST LIKE WE'RE BACK IN THAT JUNKYARD.
IT FEELS THE SAME... OR CLOSE ENOUGH FOR ME.

IT IS NOT TOO LATE FOR YOU.
REMEMBER WHAT I TAUGHT YOU. YOU CAN STILL BE A GOOD MAN.

HARDLY.
AND BESIDES, OLD FRIEND, I THINK YOU ALREADY KNOW HOW THIS IS GOING TO END.

POW!

AAAAAAGH!

NO. NOT AGAIN!

MARIA... OH GOD, I AM SO SORRY.

CRRUUUKTCH!

AAAAAAAAAAAAAH. YES.

K-K-T-C-H!
WHAT ARE WE GOING TO DO?
HUSH. QUIETLY.

IS IT TRUE?

YES. BUT I DIDN'T KNOW... ABOUT YOU. IT WAS A JOB. HE SAID IT WAS JUST A PRANK, A JOKE.
YOU WERE HIS WHORE FOR A JOKE?
STRANGE SENSE OF HUMOR YOU HAVE.

I WAS GOING TO GO TO SCHOOL WITH THE MONEY, WORK ON MY CRAFT.
IT WAS JUST TO BE THE ONE TIME.

JUST THE ONE TIME.

A GREAT DEAL OF EVIL HAS ACCOMPANIED THOSE WORDS.

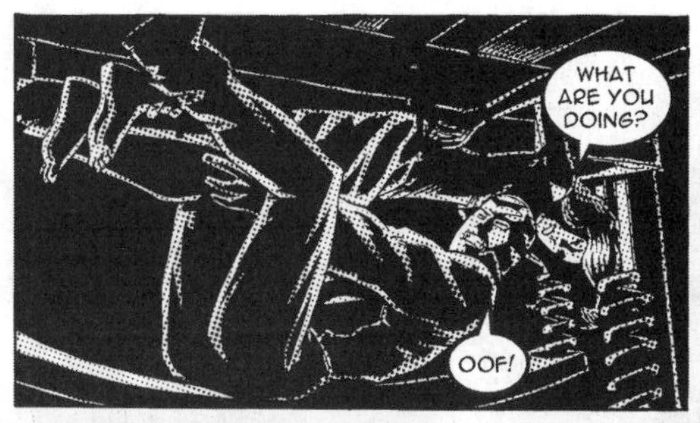
WHAT ARE YOU DOING?
OOF!

SNAP!

BUT WHY ARE YOU...?
YOU WANT TO DIE DOWN HERE AFTER ALL? I'M SORRY, YOU SHOULD HAVE MENTIONED IT.

SNAP!

SNAP!

SNAP!

NO, OF COURSE NOT, BUT...
WELL, THEN. LET'S SEE WHAT WE CAN DO.

WHAT?
YOU WILL NEED TO MOVE QUICKLY.
I DON'T HAVE MORE THAN A FEW SECONDS OF THIS IN ME.

MOVE, DAMN YOU!!!

WHY DID YOU SAVE ME?
AFTER EVERYTHING I DID TO YOU... I AM NOT WORTH SAVING.
WE ARE ALL WORTH SAVING.

BUT YOU DON'T EVEN KNOW ME. NOT THE *REAL* ME.
WE ARE ***ALL*** WORTH SAVING.

HOW CAN I HELP YOU?
GO TO THE SECOND FLOOR. CALL THE ELEVA-TOR.

I CAN'T! HE'S UP THERE. I *CAN'T*.

I'M SO SORRY. I WILL CALL THE POLICE. THEY WILL HELP YOU.
NO! THERE'S NO TIME! THE POLICE WILL NOT DO WHAT MUST BE DONE.

I'M SORRY! I JUST... CAN'T!

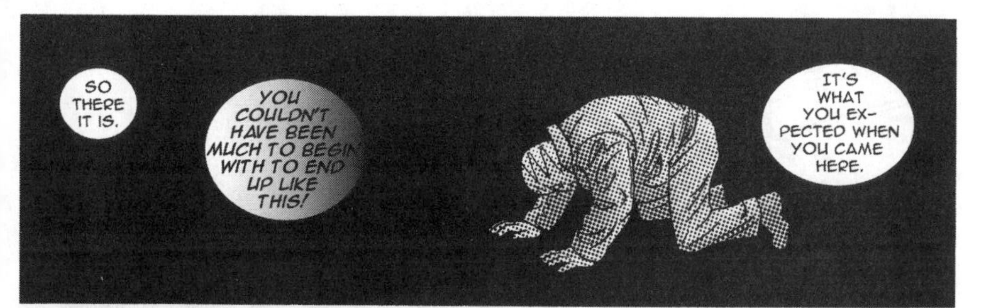
SO THERE IT IS.
YOU COULDN'T HAVE BEEN MUCH TO BEGIN WITH TO END UP LIKE THIS!
IT'S WHAT YOU EX-PECTED WHEN YOU CAME HERE.

LET GO. THIS IS WHAT YOU'VE WANTED FOR THIRTY YEARS.
JUST HOW STRONG ARE YOU?

IT'S THE HEROES WHO HAVE TO HIDE THEIR FACES.
YOU'VE EARNED IT, IF ANYONE HAS.

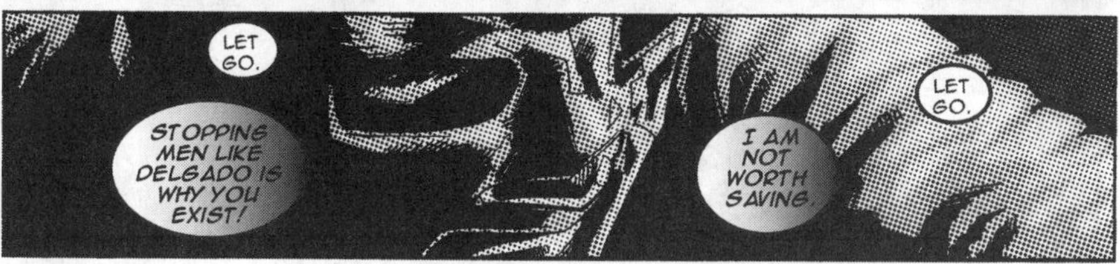
LET GO.
STOPPING MEN LIKE DELGADO IS WHY YOU EXIST!
I AM NOT WORTH SAVING.
LET GO.

LET GO.
MARIA IS WAITING FOR YOU. THE *REAL* ONE.

UP, OLD MAN.

NOT DONE JUST YET.

DING!

WELL, WELL.

ON THE FLOOR, BITCH!

LEAVE HER ALONE.

WHO THE HELL...?

BANG!

MMF!

THUD!

....
GRACIAS, MARIA.
I...
YOU'RE WELCOME.

LET'S GET OUT OF HERE!
NO.

WHAT THE HELL ARE YOU TALKING ABOUT?
EVEN HIM? NO.
WE ALL DESERVE TO BE SAVED.
EVEN HIM. BUT A MAN SUCH AS HE MUST BE SAVED, ABOVE ALL OTHER THINGS, FROM HIMSELF.

I WON'T LET YOU DO THIS!
MY WORK IS NOT YET FINISHED.
NO...

...I SUPPOSE IT IS NOT.
BANG!
RRRAAAH!
AACH!
NGAAH!
CRRAAACK!
YAARGH!
CRAAASH!

KLAANG!
KRRASH!
HOW DARE YOU?
THOK!
THUNK!
THOK!
RAAAAAR!
YOU WERE NEVER MUCH GOOD WITH YOUR LEFT HAND.

YOU SHOULD HAVE DIED IN THE ELEVATOR, OLD MAN!

KLANG!

I'M GOING TO GUT YOU.
GUT YOU, LET YOU BLEED OUT ON MY RUG!

KLAANG!

WHO THE HELL DO YOU THINK YOU ARE?

I AM TIGRE.

DIE!!!!

CRACK!

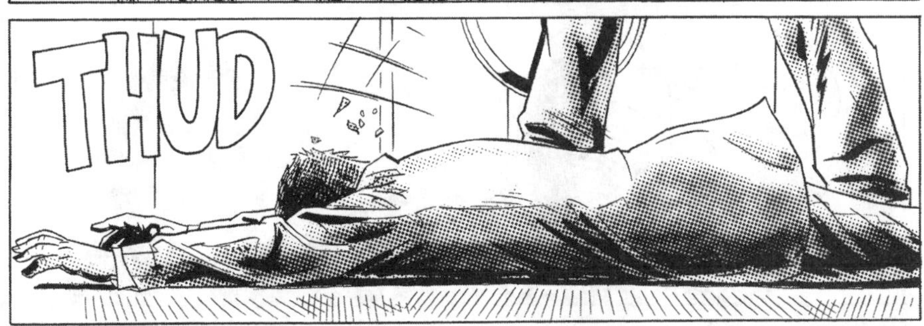
THUD

<I AM SORRY, LITTLE CONEJO.>

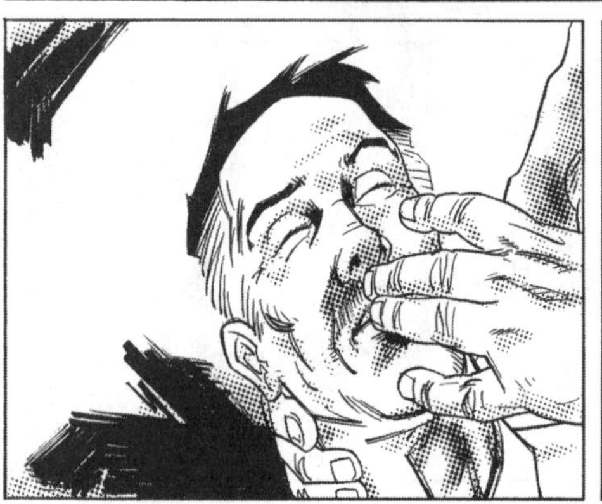

LET US GO.
YOU MAY HAVE TO HELP ME.
I AM NOT SURE I CAN STAND UP.

NO. WAIT. I HAVE AN IDEA.

WHAT ARE YOU DOING?

HE TOLD ME HE TOOK YOUR LIVER.
NOW YOU WILL TAKE HIS.

BUT YOU ARE NO DOCTOR.
HOW WILL YOU KNOW WHICH IT IS?
YES...

THEN I WILL TAKE IT ALL.

THE COOLER WILL KEEP THE ORGANS FRESH LONG ENOUGH TO GET TO A HOSPITAL.
BUT HOW WILL WE GO? I DESTROYED MY MOTORCYCLE, AND BLEW UP ALL THE CARS ON THE WAY IN.
DELGADO KEEPS... HE *KEPT* A GARAGE. WE CAN FIND SOMETHING IN THERE.
UNLESS IT'S FAST, I AM NOT SURE IT'S WORTH THE EFFORT, MARIA.
I SHOULD ALREADY BE DEAD.
VETTE
BENZ
AND I SHOULD BE A FAMOUS ACTRESS.
THINGS DON'T ALWAYS HAPPEN THE WAY THEY ***SHOULD***.

AHHH...
THAT FAST ENOUGH FOR YOU?

THIS TIME, MARIA. THIS TIME WAS DIFFERENT.
WHAT ARE YOU TALKING ABOUT?
THIS TIME?

THIS TIME...
VROOM!

TIGRE! ***TIGRE!!***
THIS TIME I... SAVED... YOU.

HARLETT HOSPITAL
ADMITTI
YOU HAVE NO IDEA HOW LUCKY YOU WERE, FINDING A LIVER DONOR THAT QUICKLY.
I HAD AN ANGEL WATCHING OVER ME.
WHATEVER YOU SAY. BUT LISTEN, TAKE IT EASY FOR ME, ALL RIGHT?
YOU'RE NOT AS YOUNG AS YOU USED TO BE.
I AM TIGRE, DOCTOR. EVERYTHING IS EASY.
NOW, PLEASE EXCUSE ME. I HAVE SOME FRIENDS WAITING FOR ME.
IT'S YOUR LIFE, DEAD MAN.

TIGRE!
HARLEM HOSPITAL
CENTER
MARTIN LUTHER KING JR. PAVILLION

The images above and to the right are some of the first Tigre shots Allen drew. It was clear early on that he was the right guy to capture the more subtle aspects of Tigre's life.

Right, detail of the slutty version of the Laocoon, from Little Pedro's office. Too cool not to get another moment in the sun.

The two character sketches above represent early takes on Tigre's look - the book could have gone a very different way.

Sample posters from Tigre's heyday - sadly unused in this project.

LITTLE PEDRO LIVES - THE GLADFELTER PROCESS

In the course of his work on the book, Allen built tiny, real-world "sets" to use as reference for scenes with tricky geography. The elevator sequence near the end of the book is one, and the showdown in Little Pedro's office is another. Here's Allen's description of how it worked:

"Here we have a demonstration of a series of steps I took to produce a scene that took place in a small office with 4 characters interacting within.

I found that blocking the scene and getting the placement of the furniture and props and characters was too confusing to maintain good continuity through the sequence, which was several pages long. So I hit on the idea of constructing a scale model set to use as a reference tool.

I made the room and furniture out of foam core at 1/12 scale, and used a combination of action figures, clay models and a live "actor" (no, he's not 3.75 inches tall). I took photos of the room using my digital camera, dropped the photos of my friend into place using Photoshop, and then combined them to make a photo layout that I then used to produce the page. I think it worked quite well. The room, and the size and placement of the characters and props, are all convincing. Voila - scene, consider yourself SOLD."

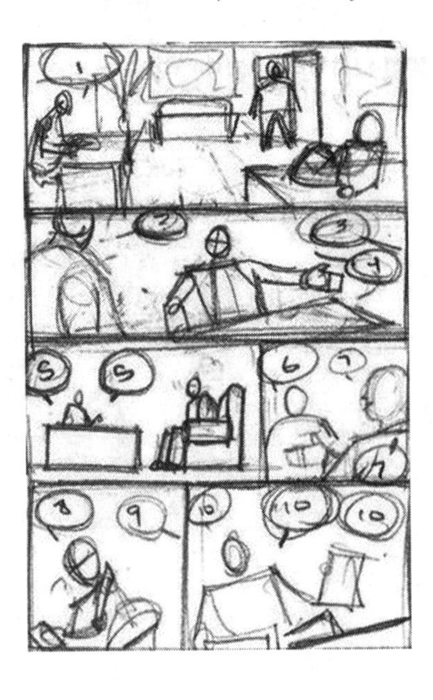

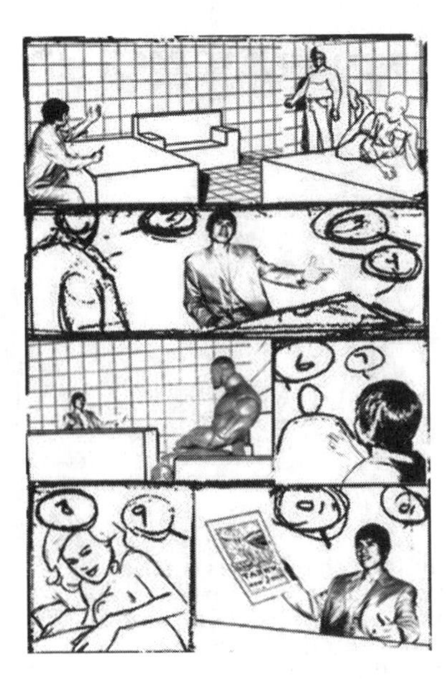

Another interesting thing to note about these pages-in-progress: the original, scripted intent was to decorate the walls of Little Pedro's office with an endless mural of pornography. The thought was that LP obssessively cut his favorite images out of skin mags and pasted them up on his walls as a sort of tribute to his own virility.

Ultimately, the finished images just looked a little busier than we deemed necessary. We decided to stick with the Little Pedro-icized versions of famous works of art that ended up in the final version of the scene.

Pinup by Scott Forb

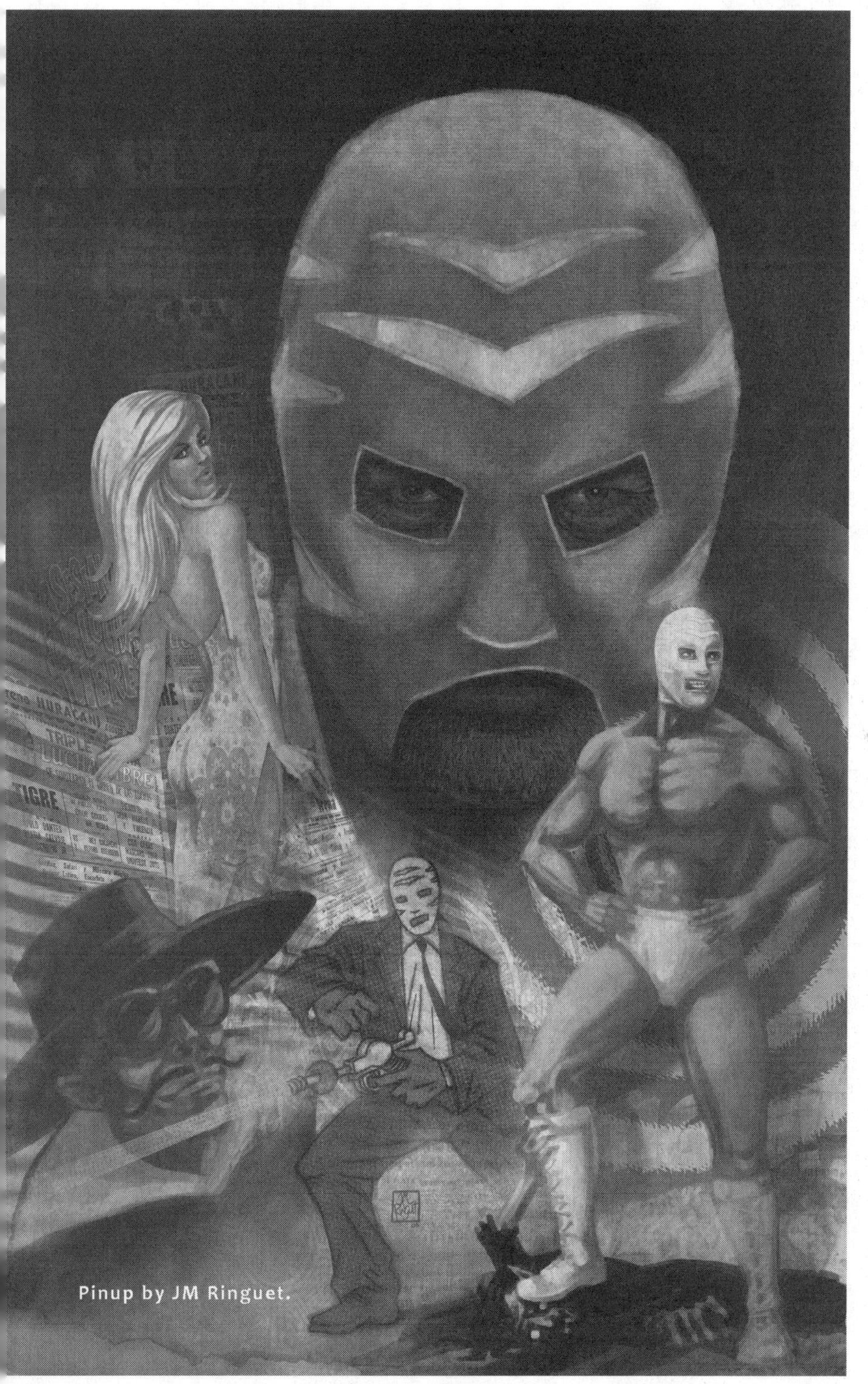

Pinup by JM Ringuet.

BIOS

CHARLES SOULE (writer) lives in New York City. He has been to Mexico twice, and has been known to wear a mask on special occasions. His record as a professional wrestler is laughable.

csoule@rocketmail.com

ALLEN GLADFELTER (artist) lives in Boise, Idaho. He has been an elementary school art teacher, freelance illustrator, graphic designer and storyboard artist.

He has worked in museums, galleries, comic book stores, picture frame shops and has done a fair amount of busking. Throughout, he has been a cartoonist.

Allen has worked as the editorial cartoonist for the Idaho Press Tribune and feature cartoonist with the Boise Weekly. Beyond the newspaper world, Allen has illustrated a number of small-press comic books including "Tex" with Joshua Dysart, "Like That" with Patrick Rills, "The Lost Tribe" with Benjamin Raab and "Comiculture" with Steve Buccellatto. Allen loves comics.

rattlinbone@yahoo.com

PAUL ADAM (covers) lives in Austin, Texas. Currently working as a concept artist for Bioware, he has also done illustration and concept design work forDisney Interactive, Petroglyph Studios and worked as an animator on the Stephen Linklater film “A Scanner Darkly.” Paul is a prince among men.

killersquirrelz@gmail.com

JOHN RUBIO (logo) lives in Austin, Texas. For more than a decade, John has worked in almost every facet of visual media including print design, marketing, advertising, video, web design, brand, multimedia, illustration, cartooning and animation.
He also knows karate.

rubio@johnrubio.com